D1551488

A Practical Guide for Disciples

A Practical Guide for Disciples

by
John MacArthur, Jr.

"GRACE TO YOU"
P.O. Box 4000
Panorama City, CA   91412

Contents

These Bible studies are taken from messages delivered by Pastor-Teacher John MacArthur, Jr., at Grace Community Church in Panorama City, California. These messages have been combined into an 8-tape album titled *A Practical Guide for Disciples*. You may purchase this series either in an attractive vinyl cassette album or as individual cassettes. To purchase these tapes, request the album *A Practical Guide for Disciples*, or ask for the tapes by their individual GC numbers. Please consult the current price list; then, send your order, making your check payable to:

The Master's Communication
P.O. Box 4000
Panorama City, CA 91412

Or call the following toll-free number:
1-800-55-GRACE

1
Principles for an Effective Missionary— Part 1

Outline

Introduction
A. The Theme of Matthew's Gospel
  1. The verification
  2. The responses
    a) Of the people
    b) Of the leaders
  3. The transition
B. The Training of Jesus' Disciples
  1. The mission
  2. The motive

Lesson
I. A Divine Commission (v. 5*a*)
  A. The Call of Christ
    1. A direct commission
    2. An indirect commission
      a) A strong desire
      b) Confirmation from the church
      c) An open door
  B. The Command of Christ
    1. Defining the command
      a) In secular Greek texts
      b) In the New Testament
    2. Determining the response
II. A Central Objective (vv. 5*b*-6)
  A. Regarding the Gentiles
  B. Regarding the Samaritans
  C. Regarding the Israelites

Introduction

Matthew 10:5-15 is our text for this study: "These twelve Jesus sent forth, and commanded them, saying, Go not into the way of the Gentiles, and into any city of the Samaritans enter not; but go, rather, to the lost sheep of the house of Israel. And as ye go, preach, saying, The kingdom of heaven is at hand. Heal the sick, cleanse the lepers, raise the dead, cast out demons; freely ye have received, freely give. Provide neither gold, nor silver, nor copper in your purses, nor a bag for your journey, neither two coats, neither shoes, nor yet a staff; for the workman is worthy of his food. And into whatsoever city or town ye shall enter, inquire who in it is worthy, and there abide till ye go from there. And when ye come into an house, greet it. And if the house be worthy, let your peace come upon it; but if it be not worthy, let your peace return to you. And whosoever shall not receive you, nor hear your words, when ye depart out of that house or city, shake off the dust of your feet. Verily I say unto you, It shall be more tolerable for the land of Sodom and Gomorrah in the day of judgment, than for that city."

A. The Theme of Matthew's Gospel

Matthew's message is that Jesus of Nazareth is the Messiah—God in human flesh. He is the promised King, Savior, and Deliverer. He came to fulfill the promises and covenants of the Old Testament and to redeem the world.

1. The verification

In the first nine chapters of his gospel, Matthew amassed evidence verifying his claim about Jesus. Christ's genealogy, birth, homage from Eastern kings,

8

perceived threat to Herod, preaching, teaching, miracles, power, and words prove that He is the Messiah.

2. The responses

Chapter nine concludes with some responses to those truths.

a) Of the people

Matthew 9:31 says, "They, when they were departed, spread abroad his fame in all that country." Christ's fame began to spread everywhere.

b) Of the leaders

However, the Pharisees said, "He casteth out demons through the prince of the demons" (v. 34). The religious leaders came to an inaccurate conclusion based on inaccurate reasoning.

Yet verse 35 says, "Jesus went about all the cities and villages, teaching in their synagogues, and preaching the gospel of the kingdom, and healing every sickness and every disease among the people."

3. The transition

An important transition occurs in Matthew 9:36: "But when he saw the multitudes, he was moved with compassion on them, because they were faint." The people were beaten and bruised by their own leaders, who had imposed on them a false, legalistic system of religion that denied the truth of God. Verse 36 explains they "were scattered abroad, as sheep having no shepherd."

Seeing the vastness and lost state of the multitude, Jesus remarked to His disciples, "The harvest truly is plenteous, but the laborers are few" (v. 37). "Harvest" is a reference to the recipients of God's ultimate judgment. He could see this mass of lost, disoriented, weary people moving like sheep to the slaughter. He knew that few could warn them and that He had to enlist others to assist Him. So He asked the disciples to pray for more workers (v. 38). Then in Matthew 10, Jesus makes them the answer to their own prayers. There is great integrity in prayer when you are willing to be the answer—and the disciples were willing.

B. The Training of Jesus' Disciples

Jesus then called His twelve disciples to Himself and gave them power to minister. Matthew 10:5 says, "These twelve Jesus sent forth."

1. The mission

The disciples didn't have the qualifications you'd think they would have needed to change the world. It wasn't what they were that was important but what God made them. In the process of their training, Jesus molded them into what they needed to be to change the world.

Jesus was sending His disciples on their first training mission. For a few short weeks they would taste what they would inevitably experience as a way of life. I think of the twelve as the original missionaries—they were the first ones Jesus ever sent out.

2. The motive

Jesus was motivated to begin this training mission because of the inevitable judgment of mankind. Paul had the same motivation, saying to the Corinthians, "Knowing, therefore, the terror of the Lord, we persuade men" (2 Cor. 5:11).

Beginning in Matthew 10:5, our Lord begins to prepare the disciples for a short-term mission. Included in His instruction is timeless counsel that would benefit them for the entirety of their ministry. It also stretches beyond them to include every person the Lord sends out.

Matthew 10:5-42 can be divided into three parts: the task of the missionary (vv. 5-15), the reaction to the missionary (vv. 16-23), and the cost to the missionary (vv. 24-42). We'll begin our study with the task.

I remember reading one critic of the church who said he thought Jesus had more class than most of His agents. One of the tragedies of contemporary Christianity is that people who claim to represent Jesus Christ don't represent Him at all. If we're going to change the world with the reality of Christ, we must understand what He told His first representatives.

Lesson

I. A DIVINE COMMISSION (v. 5a)

"These twelve Jesus sent forth, and commanded them."

A. The Call of Christ

The apostles didn't volunteer (although they were certainly willing to go); they were commissioned. They were like the prophet Jeremiah, to whom the Lord said, "Before I formed thee . . . I ordained thee" (Jer. 1:5). The disciples were sovereignly called by God. They were under orders.

Mark 6:7 is a similar passage that tells us Jesus sent them two by two. He had important reasons for doing so. The apostles would be companions in times of loneliness, strength to one another in times of temptation, and encouragement to each other in times of despondency and persecution. They could share the responsibilities of preaching and healing. And it was well known to them that according to Scripture, anyone's testimony—including Jesus'—was to be confirmed by two or three witnesses (Deut. 17:6).

For a few weeks the apostles were official ambassadors of Christ. They, like the apostle Paul, were given the ministry as a "stewardship" (Col. 1:25, NASB*). That was such a serious responsibility that Paul said, "Woe is unto me, if I preach not the gospel" (1 Cor. 9:16). He had been given a divine commission.

*New American Standard Bible.

11

1. A direct commission

The disciples received a direct commission. The Lord told them to follow Him. That was clear. They didn't put out fleeces and pray for the Lord to show them signs (cf. Judg. 6:37-40).

2. An indirect commission

In our case God is more indirect. Young men going into ministry often ask me, "How do I know if I am called to the ministry?" I think there are three criteria that will help you know.

a) A strong desire

If you delight in the Lord, He will give you the desire of your heart (Ps. 37:4). First Timothy 3:1 says, "If a man desire the office of a bishop, he desireth a good work." That implies certain men will desire the office. God puts the same desire for ministry into men's hearts today.

b) Confirmation from the church

You may think you're called to preach, but others might not think so. You need to have the confirmation of the church. Paul implied that when he said to Timothy, "Neglect not the gift that is in thee, which was given thee by prophecy, with the laying on of the hands of the presbytery" (1 Tim. 4:14).

c) An open door

In 1 Corinthians 16:9 Paul says, "For a great door, and effectual, is opened unto me."

You need to determine whether you have the desire, the confirmation, and the opportunity for ministry. If you do and your heart is fixed on that goal, it's likely that you're being called by God.

B. The Command of Christ

According to Matthew 10:5, Jesus not only sent the disciples but also commanded them.

1. Defining the command

   a) In secular Greek texts

   The Greek word translated "command" (*parangellō*) basically means giving orders. But as we look at the usage of the word, we find several shades of meaning.

   (1) Its military sense

   Parangellō is used to describe a superior giving orders to an inferior, such as a command issued to soldiers. It's a definite statement that requires obedience.

   (2) Its legal sense

   Parangellō is used of summoning a man to court. He is bound by a legal injunction to obey and respond.

   (3) Its ethical sense

   Parangellō is also used to describe teaching morals and ethics. When you learn what is ethically right, you are bound to obey it. It becomes a matter of integrity.

   (4) Its literary sense

   Parangellō is used in connection with the rules of grammar, oratory, and literary composition. It defines exactly how something is to be done.

   (5) Its medical sense

   Parangellō is used when a doctor writes a prescription for a patient.

Each of those instances binds a man to a response.

b) In the New Testament

In the New Testament *parangellō* is used approximately thirty times, often as a term for instruction. Jesus used it to instruct a leper (Luke 5:14), to command an evil spirit to come out of a man (8:29), to instruct Jairus (8:56), and to command His disciples (9:21). In Acts it is used of the Sanhedrin's command to Peter and John to stop preaching (4:18; 5:28, 40) and of the Pharisees' command to observe the ceremonial law (15:5). Paul used it in his instruction to Timothy regarding widows (1 Tim. 5:7).

Your commission is from the Lord. You are a soldier, and He is the commander. You are in court, and He is the judge. You are the student, and He is the teacher. You are the patient, and He is the doctor.

2. Determining the response

More than anything God wants your obedience. The missionary is not a chef; he is a waiter. God doesn't want you to make the meal; He just wants you to deliver it to the table. We are servants with a divine commission.

Each of us has been commissioned in some sense— some officially as evangelists and pastors—but we all are bound to obey Christ's call to represent Him in this world. The effective missionary realizes he is under divine orders. He is committed to obeying the Word of God.

II. A CENTRAL OBJECTIVE (vv. 5*b*-6)

"Go not into the way of [belonging to] the Gentiles, and into any city of the Samaritans enter not; but go, rather, to the lost sheep of the house of Israel."

The disciples weren't to go near Gentiles or Samaritans. At this particular time, Jesus was limiting the gospel to a specific place and people, but it wasn't a permanent command. This plan illustrates how God gives people a central focus with clear and limited objectives. It's been well said that self-styled messiahs are always megalomaniacs. They want to win the world and win it now. However, our Lord wants us to focus our ministry.

A. Regarding the Gentiles

1. Matthew 8:5-12—When Jesus entered Capernaum, He was approached by a centurion whose servant was sick (vv. 5-6). A centurion was a Roman soldier who commanded a hundred men. I believe Jesus brought not only healing to that Gentile's servant but also salvation to his household (v. 10). Then Jesus said, "I say unto you that many shall come from the east and west, and shall sit down with Abraham, and Isaac, and Jacob, in the kingdom of heaven; but the sons of the kingdom [many Jewish people] shall be cast out" (vv. 11-12).

The Lord has made it abundantly clear that He will reach Gentiles. Isaiah 49:6 and 54:1-3 say Jerusalem will carry the message to all the nations.

2. Mark 16:15—Jesus said, "Go ye into all the world, and preach the gospel to every creature."

B. Regarding the Samaritans

Jewish people of Jesus' day despised Samaritans. It was one thing to be a Gentile, but the Jews viewed Samaritans as corrupt half-breeds because they were a mixture of Jew and Gentile. Intermarriage is an unforgivable crime in the minds of many Jewish people even today. But Jesus was more compassionate.

1. The woman at the well (John 4:5-42)

A Samaritan woman living in the city of Sychar was the first person recorded in Scripture to whom Jesus announced that He was the Messiah. She had had many husbands and at the time was living with a man who wasn't her husband. Yet it was to her that He revealed He was the Messiah.

2. The Good Samaritan (Luke 10:30-37)

When Jesus taught that we should love our neighbors, He used a Samaritan as a positive illustration.

However, the Samaritans weren't perfect. They did many things to inflame the hatred of the Jews. For example, the first-century historian Josephus tells us that about twenty years before the time of Christ Samaritans stole into the Temple in the middle of the night during Passover and threw corpses around the Temple enclosure, thus polluting it (*Antiquities of the Jews* 18.2.2).

C. Regarding the Israelites

1. The apostles' ministry to Israel

I see three reasons for Christ's limiting the disciples' ministry "to the lost sheep of . . . Israel" (Matt. 10:6).

a) Israel's special place

The Jews were God's chosen people. The covenants, the promises, and the law were given to them. According to God's plan, they were to be offered the kingdom first. John the Baptist came to them and said, "Repent; for the kingdom of heaven is at hand" (Matt. 3:2). That meant it was imminent and available. Then Jesus Himself came and said the same thing (Matt. 4:17). Now Jesus was commanding the disciples to give the people the same message. Had the Jewish nation embraced their Messiah, His internal rule in their hearts and His external rule on earth would have come together at that time.

The Jews were the people through whom the rest of the world was to be blessed (Gen. 12:3). John 4:22 says, "Salvation is of the Jews." That doesn't mean salvation was only for them, but they were to be emissaries of God's grace to all. The nations were supposed to come to see the Messiah in Jerusalem, the launching point for world evangelism.

The disciples were to go to the people of Israel first. That was Paul's priority, too (Rom. 1:16). Although he was a missionary to the Gentiles, he always went to the synagogue first.

b) The apostles' background

The disciples were barely up to the task of reaching their own people, let alone ready to reach the Gentiles and Samaritans. They couldn't instantly overcome their lifelong biases and prejudices toward them. With the exceptions of Peter's declaration to a God-fearing man named Cornelius (Acts 10) and Philip's witness to an Ethiopian eunuch (Acts 8), no one really witnessed to the Gentile world until the ministry of Paul.

Paul was of the tribe of Benjamin, zealous for the law and trained under Gamaliel—a highly respected rabbi. He came from a Gentile area and was familiar with Gentile culture. As a result, he was able to bridge the gap to reach the Gentiles. However, the disciples weren't up to that task—they didn't have that background, so they couldn't build the bridges. If they had gone to the Gentiles or Samaritans first, they never would have been able to come back to the Jews. The Jews would have written them off as men who had concocted a Gentile-Samaritan religion.

c) Jesus' focused objective

A good commander knows he must limit his objectives, especially when his options are endless. Therefore Jesus gave the disciples a specific target: "the lost sheep of the house of Israel" (Matt. 10:6; cf. Matt. 9:36).

2. Jesus' ministry to Israel

Jesus never went to the Gentiles Himself—His ministry was almost exclusively to the Jews. In Matthew 15:24 He says, "I am not sent but unto the lost sheep of the house of Israel." They were His focus while He was on earth.

Clearing up a Frustrating Ministry

One thing that will frustrate people in ministry is the lack of a clear objective. We are easily diverted without one. I have gone to mission fields and talked with missionaries who have been in service for a long time. I find that many of them are doing a little of everything, and I wonder if they are accomplishing anything. Sometimes they don't have a clear objective. An effective ministry has a clear objective. Know your gifts. Discover what God has equipped you to do, and follow the desires of your heart.

My grandfather taught my dad and in turn my dad taught me that most people never do anything well. If you learn to do one thing well, you will be way ahead of most people. Find the one thing God wants you to do, and do it. Although people frequently ask me to do various things, I have to remember that God has called me to *preach*.

Certainly there are other needful areas of ministry. But the Lord will take care of them through the efforts of others. He's not asking any one person to do it all. If you take care of the depth of your ministry, He'll take care of the breadth of it. In churches with many ministries, many people find themselves lost in the middle. They eventually end up doing nothing or a little of everything. That isn't God's plan. Do one thing, and do it well!

Our Lord clearly kept in mind the focus of His ministry:

a) John 5:36—"The works which the Father hath given me to finish, the same works . . . I do."

b) John 4:34—"My food is to do the will of him that sent me."

c) Matthew 9:13—"I am not come to call the righteous, but sinners to repentance."

Effective ministry requires focus.

III. A CLEAR MESSAGE (v. 7)

"As ye go, preach, saying, The kingdom of heaven is at hand."

A. Declaring the Message

The kingdom of heaven can be seen three ways: in conversion, when we enter the kingdom; in consecration, when we live out the kingdom (cf. Rom. 14:17); and in consummation, when the kingdom comes to earth in its millennial form.

Jesus taught His disciples that He is Lord and that everyone needs to submit to and obey Him. After His resurrection, Jesus taught them about the kingdom for forty days (Acts 1:3).

B. Confusing the Message

I grieve in my heart over the befuddled condition of Christianity today—our message is anything but clear. On a plane trip to a pastors' conference in Chicago, I sat next to a pastor who gave me a demonstration regarding our muddled message. He wrote several things on a piece of paper. He handed it to me and said, "What does this say?" The paper had scribble written on top of more scribble. I said, "I don't know what it says." He then said, "What was my original message to you?" I said, "I don't have a clue." He said, "Take a piece of paper." I did. He said, "Write the word *Christ*. That was my original message. On top of that write *Baptist, Presbyterian, Lutheran, Episcopal, Pentecostal, charismatic, dispensational, fundamentalist, liberal, Protestant.*" He gave me about twelve other words to write. He said, "If you gave that to an unbeliever, he wouldn't know what the original message was." That's our problem: we often obscure the central message.

The message of Christianity can seem confusing when one listens to different preachers. Many of them preach all kinds of doctrine. The average unbeliever who turns on the television finds such a disparity that it is virtually impossible for him to discover the real message.

The Confusion of Bigotry

I was traveling with a team in Mississippi, preaching Christ in black high schools at the time Martin Luther King, Jr. was assassinated. One night after finishing an assembly, we visited a family in a rural area. When we left, we noticed someone following us.

We were in the middle of nowhere on a dirt road about ten miles from where we were staying. Suddenly blue lights started flashing behind us, and the car pulled up beside me, so I stopped the car. A great big man wearing a sheriff's badge got out and said, "You went through a stoplight." I said, "There are no stoplights around here. You must be mistaken." He said, "I'm not mistaken. You went through a stoplight." I said, "I didn't go through a stoplight." When he reached for a club in his belt, I said, "You're right—I went through a stoplight." I decided I'd better not argue about it! He then said, "Follow me. We're going to the jail."

We followed him for ten miles to the jail. He took us in and collected our money as collateral. He asked, "What are you telling kids in your school meetings? Do you tell them about civil rights?" I said, "No." Then he asked if we were telling them about marches, protests, or boycotts. I said no to all those things. Then I said, "We're telling them about Jesus Christ. We would be happy to tell you about Him, too." He said, "I'm the Sunday school superintendent. I don't need to hear about Him." There were many people like him in that area who called themselves ministers but were not talking about Christ and the kingdom of heaven.

Satan is not stupid. The best way to render the gospel ineffective is to make sure no one knows what it is.

C. Being Committed to the Message

Our message is this: the kingdom of heaven is at hand. The rule and reign of God is imminent and available to every person. Our focus must not be distracted. I wish every time we opened our mouths something about the kingdom would come out. We don't know how much time we have before the Lord comes, so we need to be proclaiming the kingdom with urgency.

Focusing on the Facts

1. What is the main theme of Matthew's gospel? What evidence does he give to verify his claim (see pp. 8-9)?
2. How did people respond to the truths about Christ (see p. 9)?
3. What does "the harvest" refer to in Matthew 9:37? What did Jesus want to do regarding the harvest (vv. 9:37-38; see p. 9)?
4. What motivated Jesus to send the disciples on their training mission (see p. 10)?
5. What is one of the tragedies of contemporary Christianity (see p. 11)?
6. Why did Jesus send the disciples on their mission two by two (see p. 11)?
7. The disciples received a direct commission from the Lord. How can you know if you are called to the ministry today (see p. 12)?
8. What are the different meanings of the Greek word *parangellō?* Explain each (see pp. 13-14).
9. Why is it important that the call of God be binding on our lives (see p. 14)?
10. What was God's plan for the Gentiles (see pp. 14-15)?
11. What did the Jews have against the Samaritans (see p. 15)?
12. What are three reasons Jesus sent the disciples only to Israel and not to the Gentiles or Samaritans? Explain each (see pp. 16-17).
13. Why was Paul so effective in presenting the gospel to the Gentile world (see p. 17)?
14. What was the central objective of the ministry of Christ (see p. 17)?
15. What is one reason people become frustrated in their ministries (see p. 18)?
16. What message do Christians need to be preaching to the world (see p. 18)?
17. In what three ways does the kingdom of heaven come to man (see p. 18)?
18. Why ought there be a sense of urgency in communicating the message of Christianity to the world (see p. 20)?

1. Perhaps you want to know if you're being called into a particular ministry. Review the three criteria for knowing the call of God (see p. 12). Do you have a strong desire for this ministry? Are there others in your church who believe you are capable of handling the demands that the ministry would require of you? Do you have the time and availability that this ministry would require? Take those questions to God. If you answer affirmatively to each of them, God may well be calling you into that ministry.

2. Jesus Christ commanded all Christians to be His witnesses in the world. Have you regarded that command as binding for you, or have you thought other Christians could do the witnessing? Read 2 Corinthians 5:18-21. What ministry has God given to each of us? How should we be representing Him to the world? What do you need to do to start fulfilling that role?

3. Do you find that you don't have clear objectives in the ministries you are involved in? To help develop a central objective, answer the following questions: How has God equipped you in the area of spiritual gifts (see Rom. 12:4-8; 1 Cor. 12:4-11; Eph. 4:11-13; 1 Pet. 4:10-11)? What do you desire to see accomplished in your ministry? What opportunities do you now have to minister to others? Based on your answers, where should you direct your energy? Once you determine your direction, stick with it!

2
Principles for an Effective Missionary— Part 2

Outline

Review
I. A Divine Commission (v. 5*a*)
II. A Central Objective (vv. 5*b*-6)
III. A Clear Message (v. 7)

Lesson
IV. Appropriate Credentials (v. 8)
    A. The Signs
    B. Their Significance
       1. A display of compassion
         a) Revealing the heart of God
         b) Revealing the heart of the merciless
       2. A display of power
       3. A display of unselfishness
         a) The contrast
           (1) Exorcists
           (2) Doctors
           (3) Sorcerers
         b) The free gift
V. Faith in God's Provision (vv. 9-10)
    A. The Order (vv. 9-10*a*)
    B. The Principle (v. 10*b*)
VI. An Attitude of Contentment (v. 11)
    A. Look for the Righteous (v. 11*a*)
    B. Remain with the Righteous (v. 11*b*)
VII. An Emphasis on Those Who Are Receptive (vv. 12-13*a*)
    A. Find the Open Hearts
    B. Find the Hungry Hearts

VIII. A Departure from Those Who Are Contemptuous (vv. 13b-15)
  A. Remove Your Blessing (v. 13b)
  B. Leave Their Presence (v. 14)
  C. Be Aware of Their Coming Judgment (v. 15)

Conclusion

Review

In Matthew 10:5-15 we see our Lord sending out His disciples on an evangelistic mission. The experience they would gain would help prepare them for their permanent ministry after they received the Holy Spirit. Our Lord was in the process of discipling them— building them up so they could reach their generation with the gospel.

This mission was a key stage in their training. They would get a taste of what it would be like to evangelize the lost, leave the protective care of the Shepherd, and go out into the world. Although they were unqualified from a worldly perspective, Jesus had poured His power into them, enabling them to change the world (Matt. 10:1).

As Jesus sent them out, He gave them principles for their mission. They are principles we all need to know if we're to represent Jesus Christ accurately.

  I. A DIVINE COMMISSION (v. 5a; see pp. 11-14)

  "These twelve Jesus sent forth, and commanded them."

  II. A CENTRAL OBJECTIVE (vv. 5b-6; see pp. 14-18)

  "Go not into the way of the Gentiles, and into any city of the Samaritans enter not; but go, rather, to the lost sheep of the house of Israel."

  III. A CLEAR MESSAGE (v. 7; see pp. 18-20)

  "As ye go, preach, saying, The kingdom of heaven is at hand."

24

IV. APPROPRIATE CREDENTIALS (v. 8)

"Heal the sick, cleanse the lepers, raise the dead, cast out demons; freely ye have received, freely give."

When you preach the truth about Christ, why should people believe that what you say is really from God? Why should people have believed the twelve when they said that the kingdom of heaven was at hand and that Jesus of Nazareth was the Messiah? When you go to the doctor and he diagnoses an illness, you believe him because he has a diploma hanging on the wall that says he graduated from medical school. That's his credential. When you hire someone to work for you, you make sure he has had the proper training for the work you expect him to perform.

But how would you have dealt with a preacher when there weren't any seminaries? How would you know he had the right message? The disciples were hardly a part of the existing religious establishment. They hadn't been educated in the right place—they were from Galilee, not Jerusalem. They didn't belong to any of the right groups—they weren't Pharisees, Sadducees, Essenes, or Zealots. There wasn't yet any New Testament to use as a standard. Nevertheless they did have the right credentials.

A. The Signs

Verse 8 says, "Heal the sick, cleanse the lepers, raise the dead, cast out demons; freely ye have received, freely give." Those were the credentials of the apostles, and they were convincing enough to identify them as representatives of God.

In 2 Corinthians 12:11-12 the apostle Paul says, "In nothing am I behind the very chiefest apostles, though I be nothing. Truly the signs of an apostle were wrought among you in all patience, in signs, and wonders, and mighty deeds." The credentials of an apostle were signs, wonders, and mighty deeds. Mighty deeds were miracles that created wonder—wonder that pointed to God as the source of the miracles.

A blind man Jesus healed said to the Pharisees questioning him, "Here is a marvelous thing, that ye know not from where he is, and yet he hath opened my eyes. . . . Since the age began was it not heard that any man opened the eyes of one that was born blind" (John 9:30, 32). It was obvious where Jesus came from—He came from God.

B. Their Significance

If the miracles were intended only to confirm God's servants, it would have been unnecessary for them to perform the kinds of miracles they did. They could have leaped tall buildings in a single bound. They could have disappeared and then reappeared somewhere else. They could have shot up in space, flown over the city, and swooped over buildings. Why did they perform the kinds of miracles they did?

1. A display of compassion

The first credential is: "heal the sick, cleanse the lepers" (Matt. 10:8). The disciples healed people not just for the sake of the miracle but to show compassion and mercy on people in need.

a) Revealing the heart of God

God cares for people who hurt and suffer, who are poor and sick. The miracles dramatized the mercy of God. An important element of the coming kingdom will be the eradication of disease.

Jesus always had great concern for the poor and ailing. When John the Baptist's disciples asked if Jesus really was the Messiah, He said to them, "Go and show John . . . the blind receive their sight, and the lame walk, the lepers are cleansed, and the deaf hear, the dead are raised up, and the poor have the gospel preached to them" (Matt. 11:4-5). Jesus is verified as God's Messiah because He revealed the compassionate, merciful heart of God.

One who truly represents Jesus Christ gives himself to the poor, the hurting, the needy, and the down-trodden. When people claim to represent Jesus Christ yet devote themselves to the rich and famous, I wonder about the reality of their claim. They are under the illusion that the kingdom of God is advanced only by the rich, but they are wrong.

The Old Testament repeatedly underscores the importance of the poor and needy.

(1) Psalm 9:18—"The needy shall not always be forgotten; the expectation of the poor shall not perish forever."

(2) Psalm 12:5—"For the oppression of the poor, for the sighing of the needy, now will I arise, saith the Lord; I will set him in safety."

(3) Psalm 35:10—"All my bones shall say, Lord, who is like unto thee, who deliverest the poor from him who is too strong for him, yea, the poor and the needy from him that spoileth him?"

(4) Psalm 140:12—"I know that the Lord will maintain the cause of the afflicted, and the right of the poor."

(5) Isaiah 41:17—God comes to the rescue of those who are hurting.

b) Revealing the heart of the merciless

In contrast to the representatives of God, worldly people do not manifest the compassion of God.

(1) The indictment of Scripture

The Old Testament says that wicked men op-
press the poor (Ezek. 18:12), sell them (Amos
2:6), tread upon them (Amos 5:11), grind their
faces (Isa. 3:15), persecute them (Ps. 10:2), and
defraud them (Amos 8:5-6). On the contrary,
God cares for them. He doesn't forget them (Ps.
9:18). He hears their cry (Ps. 69:33), maintains
their rights (Ps. 140:12), delivers, protects, ex-
alts, and provides for them (Ps. 35:10; 12:5;
107:41; 68:10). Psalm 14:6 says, "The Lord is his
refuge."

False prophets and teachers are merciless and
have no compassion. They use and abuse people. Jesus warned of people like that: "Beware
of the scribes, who love to go in long clothing,
and love salutations in the market places, and
the chief seats in the synagogues, and the up-
permost places at feasts; who devour widows'
houses" (Mark 12:38-40). Some religious leaders
actually extorted from the poor. Some people
today who claim to love Christ will do anything
for money, including robbing from widows
who have nothing. They have no thought for
the needy.

(2) The indictment of a reporter

I was interviewed by a reporter who had sur-
veyed Christian leaders across America. He was
extremely disillusioned. He said, "I've talked to
conservative and liberal Christians alike. Out of
all those I interviewed, I found one person who
I thought was more like Christ than any of the
others. He believes in God and Christ, but he
doesn't believe that all of the Bible is necessarily
inspired. He is not nearly as evangelical as
many, but his entire life is given to caring for
people who are poor, oppressed, and needy."

28

What a sad indictment of Christianity! He talked to a lot of people who had the right message but cared more for the rich and famous, whereas the one who impressed him didn't have the right message but manifested the right attitude.

We can't heal the sick or cleanse the lepers—we no longer have the apostolic gifts, which were limited to the apostolic era (cf. Heb. 2:1-4). But we can still show the divine compassion those miracles demonstrated.

2. A display of power

The second credential is: "raise the dead, cast out demons" (Matt. 10:8). I can't raise the dead or cast out demons, and neither can you. Today no one has the power and authority our Lord and His apostles had over demons and death. However, a true representative of Christ is marked by God's power. False teachers and apostles are impotent (Jer. 5:13). Jesus told the leaders of Israel that they didn't know the power of God (Matt. 22:29). They were impotent to change anyone's life, even their own.

A true representative of God manifests power—not to raise those who are physically dead but to redeem those who are spiritually dead through the gospel of Christ. When the apostles went forth, they went in the power of God (Luke 9:6-10; Acts 3:1-10).

3. A display of unselfishness

The third credential is: "freely ye have received, freely give" (Matt. 10:8). If you have compassion and power in your ministry, it is only by the grace of God. No one gets it by going to Bible college or seminary or by being ordained. Since we paid nothing for our power, we shouldn't charge anything to exert it. Show me someone who truly represents Jesus Christ, and I will show you someone who is not in it for personal gain.

a) The contrast

(1) Exorcists

Jewish exorcists were common in the time of Christ. When people were demon-possessed or had members of their family who were demon-possessed, they would go to the exorcists for deliverance. Ultimately those exorcists produced no results because the people were demon-possessed because of their sin, and the exorcists couldn't do anything about that. Nevertheless, people would pay great amounts of money for those exorcisms.

(2) Doctors

Medical doctors at that time would charge great amounts of money for physical healing.

(3) Sorcerers

The apostles had the power of God to cast out demons instantaneously. They could heal the sick and raise the dead. Simon Magus, a sorcerer, recognized the power the apostles had and tried to buy it (Acts 8:18-19). He was willing to pay any price because he knew that power would pay for itself a thousand times over. "But Peter said unto him, Thy money perish with thee, because thou hast thought that the gift of God may be purchased with money" (Acts 8:20). No one can buy the Holy Spirit's power.

b) The free gift

Since the gifts we have were freely given to us by God, we're to dispense them freely. First Peter 5:2 says that elders must not minister for "filthy lucre." Paul said to Timothy that when looking for an elder, he was to find a man who wasn't interested in personal gain (1 Tim. 3:3; cf. Titus 1:5, 7).

Throughout the years I have been repeatedly asked about my fee for preaching. I have been preaching for more than twenty years, yet never once in my ministry have I set a price on my gift, and I never will. The Bible says I received it freely, so I give it freely. Why should I set a price on it?

V. FAITH IN GOD'S PROVISION (vv. 9-10)

A. The Order (vv. 9-10a)

"Provide neither gold, nor silver, nor copper in your purses, nor a bag [foodbag] for your journey, neither two coats, neither shoes, nor yet a staff."

Gold, silver, and copper were different kinds of coinage. Jesus was telling the disciples not to take any money with them. They were not to assume that since they weren't going to charge people for their ministry, they would need to bring provisions for themselves.

B. The Principle (v. 10b)

"The workman is worthy of his food."

Rabbis were never to put a price on anything, demand anything, or ask a fee; the people to whom they ministered were to supply their needs. The Talmud tells us Rabbi Eliezer ben Jacob said, "If a man entertains a [rabbi] in his house and lets him enjoy his possessions, Scripture accounts it to him as if he had sacrificed the daily burnt-offering" (*Berakoth* 10b). God would bless him because he had taken care of God's servant.

Those in ministry should never be overly concerned with material things. The people of God need to acknowledge that it is their duty to support them. It is your responsibility to support those who serve you.

1. 1 Timothy 5:17-18—"Let the elders that rule well be counted worthy of double honor, especially they who labor in the word and doctrine. For the scripture saith,

31

Thou shalt not muzzle the ox that treadeth." If you want the animal to work, you have to feed it.

2. 1 Corinthians 9:14—"They who preach the gospel should live of the gospel." That's not saying one should live on what he preaches but rather that he should be supported by his preaching.

A faithful worker is worthy of his hire, and God will move through people to meet his need. If you never ask for anything, seek anything, or put a price on anything, then you can accept as a gift from God whatever comes your way.

VI. AN ATTITUDE OF CONTENTMENT (v. 11)

A. Look for the Righteous (v. 11a)

"Into whatsoever city or town ye shall enter, inquire who in it is worthy."

It is fitting for Christ's representative to stay with someone of worthy character. If you were to stay in the home of dissolute, unregenerate, vile, wicked people when you preached the message of holiness, no one would believe your message. They would identify you with your unholy surroundings.

When I preached at a meeting in a certain city, arrangements were made for me to stay in a particular motel. I went to the motel after the meeting the first night and noticed that about twenty semi-trucks were parked along the street and several scantily dressed women were standing in front of the entrance. I knew I couldn't stay in that place. People would associate me with what was going on there. Jesus instructed His disciples to find a place worthy of a representative of Jesus Christ.

B. Remain with the Righteous (v. 11b)

"There abide till ye go from there."

The disciples were to stay with the worthy people the entire time they were in their city. In the past when I

32

planned to speak in a particular city, this would often happen: a dear saint would contact me and say, "Would you stay with us? We'd love to have you." And I would say yes. Often their home was a humble, little place. The food may not have been the bill of fare of a fancy restaurant, but it was nice and simple. But about two days later, someone else would say to me, "We don't know where you're staying, but we live up on the hill. And we have a suite you can stay in." I'd find myself thinking, *That would be really nice. But how do I get out of the place I'm in now?* Jesus' instruction solves that dilemma: be content with God's provision, and stay there until it's time to leave. If God had wanted me to stay up on the hill, those people would have been the first to invite me.

Paul said to Timothy, "Godliness with contentment is great gain" (1 Tim. 6:6). Some people are never content. Paul said, "I have learned, in whatever state I am, in this to be content. I know both how to be abased, and I know how to abound" (Phil. 4:11-12).

VII. AN EMPHASIS ON THOSE WHO ARE RECEPTIVE (vv. 12-13a)

"When ye come into an house, greet it. And if the house be worthy, let your peace come upon it."

When the disciples found a worthy house, they were to stay and minister to their gracious, hospitable hosts. Once they had established their lodging in that town, they could begin their ministry, which was to preach the gospel from house to house. Whenever they visited another home, they were to greet the people in it.

A. Find the Open Hearts

The common Jewish greeting was "shalom." It refers to wholeness, soundness, health, welfare, prosperity, well-being, blessing, and benediction from God. Jesus was telling His disciples to find a place where the people were receptive to the gospel and pour themselves into it.

B. Find the Hungry Hearts

To whom should we preach? Some suggest we should preach to the uncommitted. But that means we would reach only the periphery and would have to ignore those who are hungering and thirsting to grow. I am mandated to preach to the people who want to learn the most. I want to feed a hungry heart. Now and then I will fire out exhortations to the uncommitted. But I concentrate on feeding people who are willing to receive God's Word because they are the catalyst for changing the world.

VIII. A DEPARTURE FROM THOSE WHO ARE CONTEMPTU-OUS (vv. 13b-15)

A. Remove Your Blessing (v. 13b)

"If it be not worthy, let your peace return to you."

That was an Oriental expression signifying a withdrawal of favor or blessing. The disciples were to unbless an unworthy house. They would confront the evil in that home by removing the blessing they had pronounced upon it.

The apostle John said that if anyone comes to you bringing erroneous doctrine regarding Christ, "receive him not into your house, neither bid him Godspeed; for he that biddeth him Godspeed is partaker of his evil deeds" (2 John 10-11). Don't pronounce benedictions on people who are attempting to undermine God's truth. God's blessing is not to be thrown around indiscriminately. Nor do you want people to live under the illusion that they are truly blessed or redeemed when they are not.

B. Leave Their Presence (v. 14)

"Whosoever shall not receive you, nor hear your words, when ye depart out of that house or city, shake off the dust of your feet."

When people traveled in the time of Christ, they got covered with dust. When Jewish people traveled into Gentile country, they did not want to bring Gentile soil into Israel with them because they believed it would defile the land. So before they entered Israel, they shook the dust off themselves.

In telling the disciples to shake the dust off their feet when their message was rejected in Jewish homes or towns, Jesus was teaching them to treat the people as they would Gentiles. That's what Paul did at the synagogue in Psidian Antioch (Acts 13:45-51).

Now that doesn't mean you should reject someone right away when he or she doesn't express an interest in Christ. Many of us wouldn't be redeemed if we had been treated like that. Our example from Scripture is to woo people to Christ. In 2 Corinthians 5:20 Paul says, "We beg you in Christ's stead, be ye reconciled to God." But when our pleading is done and the clear testimony of Scripture is rejected, we should turn our attention to others.

C. Be Aware of Their Coming Judgment (v. 15)

"Verily I say unto you, It shall be more tolerable for the land of Sodom and Gomorrah in the day of judgment, than for that city."

That's fearsome judgment, considering that Sodom and Gomorrah hardly had an easy time of it. Fire and brimstone rained down on both those cities and destroyed them (Gen. 19:24-25). Jesus was saying that as bad as was the total destruction of those two cities, it would be worse for any house or city in Galilee that rejected the gospel.

That statement assumes every town or house in Galilee knew more of God's truth than Sodom and Gomorrah. When the people of a city greatly exposed to the truth of God (namely Christ Himself) reject Him, a Hebrews 6:4-6 situation exists: it is impossible for them to be renewed to repentance. When you have done your best to present the gospel, but the person or persons are unreceptive and contemptuous, don't waste your time. Divine judgment rests on that city or house.

Conclusion

What have we learned? The Lord sent out His twelve disciples two by two and gave them principles for effective ministry: a divine commission, a central objective, a clear message, appropriate credentials, faith in God's provision, an attitude of contentment, an emphasis on those who are receptive, and a departure from those who are contemptuous. Those are excellent standards for our service to Christ.

Perhaps you are thinking about going to the mission field or other Christian service full-time. If so, this message has a direct application for you. If not, remember that all believers represent Christ. Each of these principles applies to you. If God were to compare your life to those standards, would He view you as a faithful missionary? The world would never have picked any one of the twelve disciples to be missionaries. But God made them what they were and gave them the principles they needed for their mission. May we be as effective as they were.

Focusing on the Facts

1. Why could people believe what the disciples preached about the kingdom of heaven (see p. 25)?
2. What credentials did Jesus give the disciples (Matt. 10:8; see p. 25)?
3. What were the signs of an apostle? How did they point to God (2 Cor. 12:11-12; see p. 25)?
4. What did the apostolic miracles dramatize (see p. 26)?
5. How did Jesus answer John the Baptist's question regarding whether He was the Messiah (Matt. 11:4-5)? Why (see pp. 26-27)?
6. What does a true representative of God do for the poor and needy (see p. 27)?
7. How does the Lord indict the scribes in Mark 12:38-40? What did He indict them for (see p. 28)?
8. What kind of power do true representatives of Jesus Christ manifest today (see p. 29)?
9. Why did Simon want to buy the Holy Spirit from the apostles? How did Peter respond to his request (Acts 8:20; see p. 30)?

10. Why should a Christian never put a price on his ministry (see p. 30)?
11. What will you know to be true if you never ask for anything, seek anything, or put a price on anything in your ministry (see p. 31)?
12. Why did the Lord want His disciples to stay only in a home that was worthy (see p. 32)?
13. What kind of greeting were the disciples to bestow on each house in which they stayed (Matt. 10:13; see p. 33)?
14. Why should Christians concentrate their ministry on those who are receptive to the message (see p. 34)?
15. Why shouldn't Christians pronounce God's blessing on those who reject the gospel (see p. 34)?
16. Why did cities of Galilee face a more severe judgment than Sodom and Gomorrah (see p. 35)?

Pondering the Principles

1. Do you manifest compassion and mercy? How do you respond to people who are sick, poor, or needy? Do you have a tendency to shy away from them, or are you drawn to meet their needs? What was your life like before you were saved? How did your life change when Jesus Christ became real in your life? Christians have the opportunity to thank God for the mercy and compassion He has extended to them by extending mercy to someone who is hurting. Make the commitment to do so to someone this week.

2. The power that Christians have available to them through the Holy Spirit is crucial to presenting the gospel to the lost. Look up the following verses: Romans 8:11, 26; 15:13; 1 Corinthians 2:4; Ephesians 3:16; 6:17; 1 Thessalonians 1:5; 2 Timothy 1:7-8. In what ways does the Spirit apply power in the believer's life? What are the purposes of that power? What is characteristic of the gospel? Are you manifesting power in your presentation of the gospel? If not, you are probably trying to communicate the gospel apart from God's power. Seek to depend on the Spirit in all you do.

3. Read 1 Corinthians 9:14 and 1 Timothy 5:17-18. In what way are those who diligently preach the gospel to be rewarded? What is

your responsibility toward those who preach the gospel faithfully? Have you been faithful to carry out that responsibility? If not, why? Thank God for those who labor in the Word. Make the commitment in your own heart to fulfill the responsibility you have to them.

4. Do you witness more often to those who are receptive to the gospel or to those who are not? As we have learned, we need to spend the majority of our time sharing with those who are receptive. If you have shared the gospel to receptive people yet they don't make a commitment to Christ, what are some ways you can further educate them about the things of God? When you meet with initial rejection, what can you do to open up the lines of communication with those people? Take time right now to pray for those to whom you have been witnessing.

3
Sheep Among Wolves—Part 1

Outline

Introduction
A. The Sweep of Our Lord's Instructions
B. The Specifics of Our Lord's Instructions
C. Confusion Regarding Our Lord's Instructions

Lesson
I. Jesus' Opening Statement (v. 16a)
   A. The Picture
      1. The vulnerability of sheep
      2. The viciousness of wolves
   B. The Perspective
      1. An honest appraisal
      2. An honest approach
         a) What we don't say
         b) What we should say
            (1) Hardship is a reality
            (2) Persecution is a reality
II. Some Basic Questions (vv. 16b-23)
   A. Who Are the Wolves? (vv. 17a, 22a)
      1. The specific agent (v. 17a)
         a) Against the saints
         b) Against the Lord
            (1) The accusation of the Pharisees
            (2) The attack of Judas
      2. The universal agents (v. 22a)
   B. Why Are They So Vicious? (vv. 18a, 22a)

Conclusion

Introduction

In Matthew 10:16-23 Jesus says, "I send you forth as sheep in the midst of wolves; be ye, therefore, wise as serpents, and harmless as doves. But beware of men; for they will deliver you up to the councils, and they will scourge you in their synagogues, and ye shall be brought before governors and kings for my sake, for a testimony against them and the Gentiles. But when they deliver you up, be not anxious how or what ye shall speak; for it shall be given you in that same hour what ye shall speak. For it is not ye that speak, but the Spirit of your Father who speaketh in you. And the brother shall deliver up the brother to death, and the father the child; and the children shall rise up against their parents, and cause them to be put to death. And ye shall be hated of all men for my name's sake, but he that endureth to the end shall be saved. But when they persecute you in this city, flee into another; for verily I say unto you, Ye shall not have gone over the cities of Israel, till the Son of man be come."

Before Christ would send out the disciples following His resurrection and ascension, they needed to anticipate the response they would face from a hostile, Christ-rejecting world. So our Lord sent them out for a brief training mission. But before He sent them, He gave them specific instructions.

A. The Sweep of Our Lord's Instructions

The instructions our Lord gave to the twelve had a telescopic effect. Initially, they were specific. Matthew 10:6 says, "Go, rather, to the lost sheep of the house of Israel." That relates to the specific setting in which the disciples lived. However, Matthew 10:23 concludes with the coming of the Son of Man—an eschatological term used by Matthew to refer to the return of Christ. Thus Christ's instructions reach beyond the apostles to the church age and the Great Tribulation, which precedes Christ's return. That reflects the history of God's people from the time of Jesus' first coming to the time of His second coming.

B. The Specifics of Our Lord's Instructions

Matthew 10:1-15 gives us insight into the apostles. Verses 1-4 tell us who they were. Verses 5-15 give us Christ's specific instructions to them. And verses 16-23 describe how the world would react to them and how they were to react to the world.

Contained in those verses are some specifics that related only to the apostles.

1. Verse 8—"Heal the sick, cleanse the lepers, raise the dead, cast out demons." There is no indication in Scripture that they actually did raise the dead on this first, brief mission. But they would do so later in their mission after the resurrection of Christ and the coming of the Holy Spirit.

2. Verse 17—"They will deliver you up to the councils, and they will scourge you in their synagogues." That also did not happen on their first mission. They weren't persecuted until after the resurrection of Christ.

C. Confusion Regarding Our Lord's Instructions

Many people misunderstand Matthew 10:5-23. They don't understand why the disciples didn't do all the things Jesus instructed them to do, or they don't understand how and where those instructions apply. But that passage fits a common biblical pattern.

In many places in the Old Testament a prophet would make an immediate prophecy that would also be fulfilled in the distant future. For example, David would speak of an event's coming to pass or make a statement about himself personally, yet he ultimately meant the Messiah (e.g., Ps. 22). Micah 5:2 says that the Messiah would be born in Bethlehem. Verses 3-4 tell us He will reign as King of the earth. But Micah said nothing about the thousands of years between His birth and His kingdom.

It is common in prophetic literature for predictions to have both an immediate and future application. In Matthew 10:5-23 our Lord predicts the role of the apostles, but He also has in mind the role of all Christians throughout history until the Great Tribulation. That's why the disciples apparently didn't raise the dead and weren't beaten in synagogues or during their first mission.

41

I. JESUS' OPENING STATEMENT (v. 16*a*)

"Behold, I send you forth as sheep in the midst of wolves."

A. The Picture

1. The vulnerability of sheep

I am not an expert on sheep and am even less of an expert on wolves. But when I was in high school I spent a few days in the desert herding a flock of sheep. That brief experience exposed me to the helplessness, dependency, and timidity of sheep. In fact, sheep so easily panic that even a jackrabbit's jumping out from behind a bush is enough to cause a whole flock to scatter. They are extremely edgy animals. It's a good thing they're nervous because when danger does come, they are utterly helpless. The only thing they can do is run away, but they aren't built for speed.

Philip Keller wrote *A Shepherd Looks at Psalm 23* based on insights gained from his experience as a shepherd. He said that sheep need to be protected from poisonous weeds, weather, parasites, all kinds of diseases, and especially insects. In fact, certain flies lay their eggs on the mucous membranes of the sheep's nose. As the hatched larvae work their way up the nose, the sheep have been known to beat their heads against rocks or trees, sometimes until they are dead. The advanced stages of infection from those flies often cause blindness. Sometimes the sheep panic and stampede in an attempt to escape the flies. But when they get so agitated they often become exhausted, lose weight, and sometimes even die ([Grand Rapids, Mich.: Zondervan, 1970] pp. 115-16).

2. The viciousness of wolves

The most severe enemy of sheep is the predator—the flesh-eating wild animal (indicated in Matthew 10:16 as a wolf). According to Keller, "Two [wild] dogs have been known to kill as many as 292 sheep in a single night of unbridled slaughter. Ewes, heavy in lamb, when chased by dogs or other predators will slip their unborn lambs and lose them in abortions. A shepherd's loss from such forays can be appalling. One morning at dawn I found nine of my choicest ewes, all soon to lamb, lying dead in the field. . . .

"On several occasions [cougars] came in among my sheep at night working terrible havoc in the flock. Some ewes were killed outright, their blood drained and livers eaten. Others were torn open and badly clawed. . . . Some had huge patches of wool torn from their fleeces. In their frightened stampede some had stumbled and broken bones or rushed over rough ground injuring legs and bodies.

"Yet despite the damage, despite the dead sheep, despite the injuries and fear instilled in the flock, I never once actually saw a cougar on my range. So cunning and so skillful were their raids they defy description" (pp. 37, 108-9). Wolves are just as deadly.

Shepherding is a difficult profession. At the time of our Lord, the typical shepherd didn't own his sheep; he worked for the owner. If a shepherd reported the killing of a sheep, he had to show a piece of flesh from that sheep to prove that a wild animal had killed it—even if it meant pulling the evidence from the wolf's mouth! The shepherd might lose his own life if he didn't show proof. The sheep owners feared their sheep would be stolen unless they required evidence of a killing.

B. The Perspective

1. An honest appraisal

The conflict between sheep and wolves was familiar to the disciples. That they were to be sent among vicious, deadly wolves was our Lord's way of graphically illustrating the dangers of confronting a Christ-rejecting, God-hating world with the message of the kingdom.

Sometimes the wolves are among us

a) Acts 20:29—Paul said to the elders of the Ephesian church, "I know this, that after my departing shall grievous wolves enter in among you, not sparing the flock."

b) Romans 8:36—Paul here cited Psalm 44:22: "We are killed all the day long; we are accounted as sheep for the slaughter." Some people view Christians as sheep to be slaughtered.

Sometimes the wolves are outside the fold, but sometimes they are inside, masquerading as shepherds (Matt. 7:15).

In Matthew 9:38 Jesus refers to the multitude as sheep without a shepherd. However, they are like wolves when confronted with the gospel. The Good Shepherd gives His life for the sheep—He will defend us (John 10:14-15).

2. An honest approach

Jesus' honesty is refreshing. I don't believe He'd be at home with contemporary Christianity—we aren't honest enough.

a) What we don't say

We are so concerned about saving people that we are tempted to water down the gospel. Many professing Christians don't talk about repentance or confession of sin. They don't talk about the importance of humbling oneself or hungering and thirsting for righteousness. They don't talk about obedience to Christ. They don't talk about the narrow way that leads to salvation or the ultimate cost of following Christ. And when someone becomes a believer, they don't talk about going out into the world as sheep among wolves. Few of us are as honest as Jesus was.

The popular appeal today promises ease, comfort, riches, advancement, and ambition. But Jesus offers hardship and perhaps death.

b) What we should say

We must tell the truth. If we are dishonest when we explain the gospel and service to Christ, the people who respond will come to Him with false understanding. What have we gained? That will only put more people on the broad road to destruction who are deluded into thinking they are on the road to salvation (Matt. 7:13-14). We cannot water down the gospel.

(1) Hardship is a reality

When Jesus called people into His service, He warned them of the hardships to come. Giuseppe Garibaldi, nineteenth-century Italian patriot, said, "Men, I'm getting out of Rome. Anyone who wants to carry on the war against the outsiders, come with me. I can't offer you either honor or wages; I offer you hunger, thirst, forced marches, battles and death. Anyone who loves his country, follow me" (Guerzoni, *Garibaldi* [1882], I. p. 331). Prime Minister Winston Churchill, addressing the British House of Commons on May 13, 1940, following the battle of Dunkirk, said, "I would say to the House, as I said to those who have joined this Government, 'I have nothing to offer but blood, toil, tears, and sweat.'" Similarly, our Lord offers blood, sweat, tears, hunger, thirst, and death.

(2) Persecution is a reality

Life is tough on the mission field, but it's also tough as a missionary at home. If you're not suffering much persecution, it could be because you are not definitive about your faith. Second Timothy 3:12 says, "All that will live godly in Christ

Jesus shall suffer persecution," But God also may be graciously allowing you a time of respite. Somewhere in the world the church is suffering persecution. One day we may experience it here.

A woman once told me about her job, in which she counseled people with social problems. The only solution she found to their problems was Jesus Christ. But her employers instructed her not to speak of Christ to anyone. She wanted to know what I thought she should do. I told her she had to decide whether to obey God or men (Acts 5:28-32). She decided to obey God, even if it meant losing her job.

If we are definitive about our faith, there will be a price to pay. You cannot confront a God-hating world and expect no reaction. But much of our Christianity is locked up within church walls. I often wonder if the world even knows who we are.

II. SOME BASIC QUESTIONS (vv. 16b-23)

A. Who Are the Wolves? (vv. 17a, 22a)

1. The specific agent (v. 17a)

"Beware of men."

a) Against the saints

Men are the wolves. It's true we wrestle "against principalities, against powers, against the rulers of the darkness of this world, against spiritual wickedness in high places" (Eph. 6:12). Satan, the prince of the power of the air (Eph. 2:2), the ruler of the darkness of this world, is behind the demonic system. But its agents are human. Throughout the years men have imprisoned, crucified, burned, and stoned the saints of God. Men are the enemy—men who talk about the milk of human kindness yet are actually the dupes of Satan.

Matthew 5:10-11 says, "Blessed are they who are persecuted for righteousness' sake. . . . Blessed are ye, when men shall revile you, and persecute you, and shall say all manner of evil against you falsely, for my sake." It is men who do those wicked things.

b) Against the Lord

Although the disciples had avoided persecution up to this point, the Lord had not.

(1) The accusation of the Pharisees

Matthew 9 shows an escalation of hostilities. In verse 2 Jesus forgives the sin of a paralyzed man. In response, the religious leaders "said within themselves, This man blasphemeth" (v. 3). Then they approached the disciples and said, "Why eateth your Master with tax collectors and sinners?" (v. 11). Their hatred for Jesus intensified to the point that they exclaimed, "He casteth out demons through the prince of the demons" (v. 34).

(2) The attack of Judas

There was a wolf among the twelve disciples named Judas. He betrayed Jesus, thus beginning the chain of events that led to His murder.

We need to beware of men. Yet we must not forget to reach out to them and love them as God does. We are to "do good unto all men, especially unto them who are of the household of faith" (Gal. 6:10). We need to maintain a balanced attitude.

The enemy will attack through human agents. Don't be shocked when you are criticized. Don't be surprised when you are fired for articulating your faith. Don't be surprised when you're not invited to certain activities. Human agents represent the kingdom of darkness.

2. The universal agents (v. 22a)

"Ye shall be hated of all men."

47

"All men" doesn't refer to every human being who ever lived. Scripture allows for a certain amount of literary license, as when David said, "Every night I make my bed swim, I dissolve my couch with my tears" (Ps. 6:6, NASB). According to Mark 11:32, all men believed John the Baptist to be a prophet. That's obviously a general statement. So Matthew 10:22 appears to be saying that all classes, races, nationalities, and cultures of mankind throughout history will react negatively to the gospel.

The Gospel According to Romans

God is sovereign—He knows how much we can bear. He shortens the length of trials for certain people in certain places. But I believe the main reason we don't experience more overt persecution is that we have altered our message to accommodate rather than confront.

The gospel begins with this fact: men are lost. Romans 1:18 says, "The wrath of God is revealed from heaven against all ungodliness." Imagine what might happen if you began to present the gospel this way: "The wrath of God is revealed against you for your ungodliness. You know what is true of God by the creation around you. But you have turned the truth into a lie and worshiped the creature more than the Creator. God has given you up to your own lusts." That is greatly different from the way we normally present the gospel. When you preach repentance, you are actually confronting people with their sinfulness. Since men are the dupes and agents of Satan, you can count on them to react against God's message.

Only the Toughest Recruits Need Apply

When people are recruited for the ministry, they need to be reminded that they are going out as sheep among wolves. The apostle Paul understood that. In 1 Corinthians 4:9-13 he says, "I think that God hath set forth us, the apostles, last, as it were appointed to death; for we are made a spectacle. . . . We are fools for Christ's sake . . . and are naked, and are buffeted. . . . We are made as the filth of the world, and are the offscouring of all things."

48

1. "Made a spectacle"

   When a Roman general defeated another nation or city, he had the privilege of parading his army through the streets to demonstrate his triumph. At the end of the parade was a group of captives being led to certain death. That is the meaning of "spectacle." First Corinthians 4:9 in Moffat's *A New Translation* reads, "God means us apostles to come in at the very end, like doomed gladiators in the arena!"

2. "Appointed to death"

   Jesus told Peter he would die (John 21:18-19). It is believed most of the apostles were martyred.

3. "We are fools"

   The world generally viewed the apostles as fools and their message as foolishness (1 Cor. 1:23).

4. "Buffeted"

   The Greek word translated "buffeted" means "to strike someone with your fist." It was used to refer to the ill treatment of slaves.

5. "Offscouring"

   That is what would be scoured off a dirty dish.

Being an apostle was no easy ministry. Serving Christ never is.

   B. Why Are They So Vicious? (vv. 18a, 22a)

      "Ye shall be brought before governors and kings for my sake. . . . Ye shall be hated of all men for my name's sake."

      "For my name's sake" refers to all that Christ is. Believers are persecuted because of who Christ is and what He has done.

         1. Galatians 6:17—Paul said, "I bear in my body the marks of the Lord Jesus." Visible on Paul's body were the

marks and scars from the stonings, whippings, and beatings he endured. To him they represented the marks of Christ. He knew they weren't intended for him. People weren't angry with Paul; they were upset at Christ. Since they couldn't strike Christ, they got to His emissary.

2. Colossians 1:24—Paul said, "[I] fill up that which is behind of the afflictions of Christ in my flesh." Paul took blows meant for Christ.

3. Philippians 3:10—Paul prayed, "That I may know him, and the power of his resurrection, and the fellowship of his sufferings."

4. 1 Peter 4:14—Peter said, "If ye be reproached for the name of Christ, happy are ye; for the Spirit of glory and of God resteth upon you." When you stand with Christ, Satan will cause people to ostracize, criticize, condemn, and falsely accuse you. But it's truly a joy to take blows meant for Him since He took blows meant for us.

As Paul was on the road to Damascus, breathing out threats and persecuting Christians, the Lord struck him down and blinded him (Acts 9:3). Verses 4-5 say, "He fell to the earth, and heard a voice saying unto him, Saul, Saul, why persecutest thou me? And he said, Who art thou, Lord? And the Lord said, I am Jesus, whom thou persecutest." Paul had never met Jesus, and Jesus was in heaven, so how could he have been persecuting Jesus? Christ was living through His people, and when Paul persecuted His people, he persecuted Him. Paul never forgot that (Acts 22:7-8; 26:14-15).

The reason the wolves are so vicious is that they hate Christ. Jesus said, "He that is not with me is against me" (Matt. 12:30).

Conclusion

How do we react to a hostile world? I believe it will become more hostile when we are faithful to declare the truth with the honesty of our Lord and His disciples. Jesus gathered the twelve and told them He was sending them out as sheep among wolves. Later He told them He would never leave or forsake them. They would win in the end (Matt. 28:20; John 14:18-19).

How the Sheep Fight Back

The sheep will defeat the wolves—not in their own strength but on the basis of Christ's power. The disciples wanted to stay close to Jesus because they knew He was their resource. He was the source of their food—He fed them on the side of the hill (John 6:1-14). He was the source of their tax money—on at least one occasion He provided it from the mouth of a fish (Matt. 17:27). He was the source of their love—He poured His love upon them and cared for them. He turned nature into a parable so that every time they saw a field, a tree, a mountain, an animal, a leaf, a flower, or a piece of grain, they instantly thought of spiritual truth. He was everything to them. When He told them He was going to go away and leave them to the wolves, they surely must have panicked. But He also told them He would send His Spirit to dwell in them. He would become their strength and power to overcome the world (John 14:1-26; 1 John 5:4-5). Through the Spirit in his life, the believer continually communes with the living Christ.

Focusing on the Facts

1. In what way do the instructions Jesus gives the disciples in Matthew 10:16-23 have impact beyond that first missionary venture (see p. 40)?
2. What were some of the specific instructions that related only to the apostles? When did some of those things actually occur (see p. 41)?
3. Why do many people misunderstand Matthew 10? What pattern was established in the Old Testament that Christ followed in His instructions in Matthew 10 (see p. 41)?
4. What are some of the dangers sheep face? What is the most severe danger? Why (see pp. 42-43)?
5. Explain the difficulty of the shepherd's task, especially in biblical times (see p. 43).
6. What don't many professing Christians often talk about in their presentation of the gospel? What should they be talking

about? Why do we need to be totally honest in our presentation (see pp. 44-45)?

7. Who is behind the world system? Who are the agents and wolves of that system (see p. 46)?

8. What persecution did the Lord endure during His earthly life (see p. 47)?

9. What might Jesus have meant when He said, "Ye shall be hated of all men" (Matt. 10:22; see p. 48)?

10. What was the apostle Paul's attitude about being a true servant of Jesus Christ? What does each recruit need to be aware of? Explain (1 Cor. 4:9-13; see pp. 48-49).

11. Why are the wolves so vicious (Matt. 10:18, 22; see p. 49)?

12. Why should Christians be joyful in the midst of persecution (1 Pet. 4:14; see p. 50)?

13. How are the sheep to fight back (see p. 51)?

Pondering the Principles

1. Are you guilty of watering down the gospel? Look up the following verses: Matthew 5:6; 7:13-14; 2 Corinthians 7:9-10; James 4:8-10; 1 John 1:8-10; 2:3-6. To what aspect of salvation does each of those verses refer? Are those aspects part of your gospel presentation? If some are not, you need to begin to present all the truth of the gospel. What happens when people respond to only a partial presentation of the gospel? Ask God to guide you in determining all you need to say.

2. Read 1 Corinthians 4:9-13. If that were your call and your future as a servant of Christ, would you follow Him? It could be your call, especially if your faith is definitive. Spend some time in prayer. Ask God to reveal the condition of your heart in this area. Ask Him to show you anything preventing you from making a complete commitment to serve Him. If you have any fear regarding what you might face, read Romans 8:31-39. Meditate on those verses, and make them your daily prayer.

3. What is your attitude toward suffering and persecution? If necessary, would you be willing to suffer for Christ's sake? Read 1 Peter 4:1-2, 12-14 and Philippians 3:10. What are the advantages and benefits of suffering for Christ? To help you maintain the proper perspective, memorize Philippians 3:10.

4
Sheep Among Wolves—Part 2

Outline

Review
I. Jesus' Opening Statement (v. 16a)
II. Some Basic Questions (vv. 16b-23)
  A. Who Are the Wolves? (vv. 17a, 22a)
  B. Why Are They So Vicious? (vv. 18a, 22a)

Lesson
  C. How Do the Wolves Attack? (vv. 17-18, 21)
    1. Through religion (v. 17)
     a) The Jewish religion
     b) Other religions
      (1) Persecution by the Romans
      (2) Persecution by natives
      (3) Persecution by so-called Christians
      (4) Persecution by "Babylon the great"
    2. Through the government (v. 18)
     a) Persecution in the Roman Empire
     b) Persecution throughout history
     c) Persecution during the Tribulation
    3. Through the family (v. 21)
  D. How Are the Sheep to Respond? (vv. 16b-17a, 19-20, 22b-23)
    1. Be wise (v. 16b)
     a) Achieve the highest goal
     b) Avoid offending people unnecessarily
    2. Be harmless (v. 16c)
     a) Gentleness
     b) Purity
    3. Be on your guard (v. 17a)

4. Be calm (vv. 19-20)
    a) The general application to all believers (v. 19)
    b) The specific instruction for the apostles (v. 20)
        (1) The promise of divine inspiration
        (2) The implication of biblical inerrancy
5. Be patient (v. 22)
6. Be on the move (v. 23)

Conclusion

Review

In Matthew 10:16-23 the Lord Jesus Christ prepares to send the apostles into a hostile world that will reject them. They needed to know what to do, so Jesus carefully instructed them.

I. JESUS' OPENING STATEMENT (v. 16*a*; see pp. 42-46)

"Behold, I send you forth as sheep in the midst of wolves."

II. SOME BASIC QUESTIONS (vv. 16*b*-23)

A. Who Are the Wolves? (vv. 17*a*, 22*a*; see pp. 46-49)

"Beware of men. . . . And ye shall be hated of all men."

B. Why Are They So Vicious? (vv. 18*a*, 22*a*; see pp. 49-50)

"Ye shall be brought before governors and kings for my sake. . . . And ye shall be hated of all men for my name's sake."

Lesson

C. How Do the Wolves Attack? (vv. 17-18, 21)

1. Through religion (v. 17)

"Beware of men; for they will deliver you up to the councils, and they will scourge you in their synagogues."

a) The Jewish religion

"Synagogues" is the key word because it establishes a religious context. The Jewish people had synagogues (meeting places) in virtually every town and village. There the religious leaders carried out their law.

If someone violated any of the laws of Moses or rabbinical tradition, he would be brought before the local synagogue. A tribunal of twenty-three judges would render a verdict, followed by a sentencing. Frequently, the sentence was scourging. Old Testament law required that no more than forty stripes be given to each victim (Deut. 25:3), so they never gave more than thirty-nine, making sure they remained within the letter of the law. One judge would recite a passage from the Old Testament, and another would call out the number of blows to be given (cf. the Babylonian Talmud, *Makkoth* 22*b*).

Our Lord told the disciples to expect to be delivered up to "the councils," the local courts in the synagogues. The supreme court of the land was the Sanhedrin in Jerusalem.

The apostles were scourged in the synagogue (Acts 5:40). Acts 22:19 tells us that before his conversion, the apostle Paul went from synagogue to synagogue ordering Christians to be scourged for heresy. Second Corinthians 11:24 says that Paul himself was scourged five times.

Commentator William Barclay said, "It has often been true that the man with a message from God has had to undergo the hatred and the enmity of a fossilized orthodoxy" (*The Gospel of Matthew*, vol. 1, rev. ed. [Philadelphia: Westminster, 1975] p. 376). Christ was sentenced to death by religionists—the chief priests, scribes, Pharisees, and elders.

Jewish persecution of Christians continued until the destruction of Jerusalem in A.D. 70. Although individual Jewish people who come to Christ often expehence rejection and persecution from their family, there has been no wide-scale persecution of Christians by Jews since A.D. 70.

b) Other religions

Although the Bible shows that Jews once persecuted Christians, that is only a representation of religious persecution in general. There have been and will be other councils of religionists who persecute Christianity.

(1) Persecution by the Romans

The Romans increasingly became committed to emperor worship, and Christianity threatened that worship.

(2) Persecution by natives

Demons have influenced pagan people in remote areas to massacre innocent missionaries.

(3) Persecution by so-called Christians

Associated with Christianity are false teachers who devastate the church. As Paul says in Acts 20:29, "I know this, that after my departing shall grievous wolves enter in among you, not sparing the flock."

(4) Persecution by "Babylon the great"

According to Revelation 17, the worst persecution will occur during the Tribulation. Revelation 17:5 identifies the final form of world religion as "mystery, Babylon the great, the mother of harlots and abominations of the earth."

When the people from the Tower of Babel were scattered, they apparently spread the roots of false religion around the globe. By the end times it will culminate in one world religion controlled by Satan.

As John saw the vision of the future false religion, he said, "I saw the woman [the final representation of world religion] drunk with the blood of the saints, and with the blood of the martyrs of Jesus" (Rev. 17:6).

We should not be surprised by such a future. Our Lord warned of those who would come dressed in "sheep's clothing, but inwardly they are ravening wolves" (Matt. 7:15). Satan disguises himself as an angel of light, so we shouldn't be surprised if his ministers are disguised as servants of righteousness (2 Cor. 11:14). Such religion masks itself as respectable but in fact persecutes the truth. It is operated by Satan, who is a liar and a murderer.

2. Through the government (v. 18)

"Ye shall be brought before governors and kings for my sake, for a testimony against them and the Gentiles."

"For a testimony against them" could refer to standing as a living rebuke to those who persecute you. But I believe it refers literally to being brought before government officials to give your testimony. That's what happened to the apostles.

a) Persecution in the Roman Empire

The Roman government feared a slave revolt since there were approximately 20 million slaves in the empire. Slaves and freedmen could not marry because a slave wasn't considered a person. But when slaves became Christians, they were immediately confronted with the truth that in the spiritual realm there is neither slave nor free (Gal. 3:28; Col. 3:11). Therefore many Roman authorities thought Christianity was dangerous.

Sometimes the government made up charges against the Christians. They distorted the symbolic meaning of eating the flesh and drinking the blood of Christ in Communion and accused them of cannibalism. They accused them of immorality in their love feasts. They accused them of revolution because their eschatology taught that the earth would be destroyed by fire. As a result, Christians were blamed for the burning of Rome in A.D. 64. They accused Christians of disloyalty to the emperor because they wouldn't bow down to him. They also accused them of breaking up marriages and destroying the family.

The Roman Empire persecuted Christians. Most of the disciples who heard Jesus' instruction in Matthew 10 died at the hands of the government.

b) Persecution throughout history

Governments have attacked the church throughout history. In Russia, countless Christians were slaughtered after the Communist revolution. Many were slaughtered in Communist China as well. In Uganda under the government of Idi Amin, Christians suffered horrifying atrocities. Pastor F. Kefa Sempangi told about going with one of his church's elders to visit a family. They found the entire family terribly mutilated, with the exception of one small boy, who somehow was overlooked by the assassins (*A Distant Grief* [Glendale, Calif.: Regal, 1979], pp. 46-48).

c) Persecution during the Tribulation

In the Tribulation the government of the Antichrist will persecute whatever Christians are around. Revelation 13:7 tells us that after he comes to power "it was given unto him to make war with the saints, and to overcome them; and power was given him over all kindreds, and tongues, and nations." Verse 10 says he will kill them.

Christians have never been able to avoid trouble. Although governments are entities ordained by God to preserve the social structure (Rom. 13), they are also manipulated by Satan. Daniel, Isaiah, and Ezekiel saw the demonic forces behind their governments. The government of the world will persecute Christianity because Satan is the prince of this world (John 12:31).

You might think the United States will never persecute Christianity. But if the Lord tarries and we live long enough, we may see the day when our government will deny us some of the freedoms we have had in the past. Restrictions are already affecting us now.

3. Through the family (v. 21)

"The brother shall deliver up the brother to death, and the father the child; and the children shall rise up against their parents, and cause them to be put to death."

I have known of people whose families held funeral services for them when they became believers in Christ. I knew of a child who was killed because of his Christian faith. Only God knows how many people have been persecuted, betrayed, or killed by members of their own families because of their faith in Christ.

Commentator R. C. H. Lenski quoted one author as saying, "two things are stronger than natural love, the one born of hell, the other born of heaven" (*The Interpretation of St. Matthew's Commentary* [Minneapolis: Augsburg, 1943], p. 404). According to Romans 1:24-26, people forsake natural affections because they are so evil.

a) Zechariah 13:3—This will be the fate of false prophets at the return of Christ: "It shall come to pass that, when any shall yet prophesy, then his father and mother who begot him shall say unto him, Thou shalt not live; for thou speakest lies in the name of the Lord; and his father and his mother who begot him shall thrust him through when he prophesieth."

b) Matthew 10:34-37—Jesus said, "I came not to send peace, but a sword. . . . To set a man at variance against his father. . . . A man's foes shall be they of his own household. He that loveth father or mother more than me, is not worthy of me; and he that loveth son or daughter more than me, is not worthy of me."

59

c) Mark 13:12-14—Families will also be set against each other during the Tribulation. Jesus said, "Brother shall betray brother to death, and the father, his son; and children shall rise up against their parents, and shall cause them to be put to death. And ye shall be hated of all men for my name's sake; but he that shall endure unto the end, the same shall be saved. But when ye shall see the abomination of desolation, spoken of by Daniel, the prophet." That last phrase places the context of the prophecy as the middle of the Tribulation.

Christians will be persecuted because the world reacts negatively to the gospel. Members of false religions react because those religions are generated by Satan. Governments react because they are influenced by the prince of this world. And families react because they cannot tolerate a righteous individual in the midst of their unrighteousness (cf. 1 Pet. 4:3-4).

D. How Are the Sheep to Respond? (vv. 16*b*-17*a*, 19-20, 22*b*-23)

1. Be wise (v. 16*b*)

"Be ye, therefore, wise as serpents."

In Egyptian hieroglyphics the serpent is a symbol for wisdom. Many of the ancients viewed snakes as shrewd, cunning, prudent, and cautious. In Colossians 4:5 Paul says, "Walk in wisdom toward them that are outside." Christians are to be wise in dealing with the wolves of the world.

a) Achieve the highest goal

We're to say the right thing at the right time in the right place. It's our goal to discover the best means to achieve the highest goal.

b) Avoid offending people unnecessarily

We must be careful about how we approach an anti-Christian world. You can make inflammatory statements and ignite conflict, or you can use discretion.

When the Pharisees and Herodians asked Jesus if they should pay taxes, our Lord replied, "Render . . . unto Caesar the things which are Caesar's; and unto God, the things that are God's" (Matt. 22:21). He didn't compromise the truth, yet He was wise enough not to say everything that could have been said and perpetuate an argument.

Be wise. Find the best way to handle a confrontation or conflict. Don't make unnecessary trouble, and don't wreak havoc.

2. Be harmless (v. 16*c*)

"[Be] harmless as doves."

a) Gentleness

Christians are not to be intrusive, brash, or rude. We're to be harmless and gentle.

b) Purity

In Song of Solomon 5:2 the husband calls his wife "my dove, my undefiled." The dove was a symbol of purity, holiness, and innocence. Although we are to be wise, we also are to be pure. As we seek the wisest method of dealing with a problem, we should never compromise the truth. Keep your integrity, honesty, and purity. Those who represent Christ are not to cause injury or employ trickery or deceit in trying to escape from danger; they are to be wise, pure, and gentle.

(1) Luke 6:27—"Love your enemies, do good to them who hate you." To do that you must be as wise as a serpent and harmless as a dove.

(2) 1 Corinthians 9:22—Paul said, "I am made all things to all men, that I might by all means save some." We're to be flexible but must not compromise the truth in the process. Find that balance between the two.

(3) 1 Peter 2:23—When our Lord was reviled, He didn't revile in return. When His enemies abused Him on the cross, He forgave them their sin (Luke 23:34). Such was the gentleness displayed by Jesus.

3. Be on your guard (v. 17a)

"But beware."

Evil intentions lurk in the hearts of many. When I talk to the press or do a radio interview, I have to be watchful and discerning, seeking to avoid forums that attempt to discredit the gospel.

In Acts 23 we see Paul caught in such a situation. He says he stood before God with a clear conscience. The high priest "commanded them that stood by him to smite him on the mouth. Then said Paul unto him, God shall smite thee, thou whited wall" (vv. 2-3). But then Paul had to apologize (v. 5). He wasn't as alert and under control in that situation as he should have been.

Don't give the wolves an opportunity to condemn you. One of their evil intentions is to make you compromise.

4. Be calm (vv. 19-20)

a) The general application to all believers (v. 19)

"When they deliver you up, be not anxious how or what ye shall speak; for it shall be given you in that same hour what ye shall speak."

If you were arrested, you'd tend to worry about your defense. But Jesus told the disciples not to worry because He would take care of them. They didn't need to prepare a defense; they just needed to relax and stay calm. In Philippians 4:6 Paul says, "Be anxious for nothing."

Jesus gave the reason for not being anxious: "It shall be given you in that same hour what ye shall speak" (v. 19). I believe that when anyone goes before any council in the name of Jesus Christ, the Spirit of God will bring to his or her mind the right things to say. Based on what we have learned from our study of Scripture, we know the Spirit of God will be our defender.

Many of the most memorable and powerful testimonies of the great martyrs were uttered just before they were put to death. God gave them a special presence of mind and clarity of thought to present a testimony more powerful than they would otherwise have been able to give.

b) The specific instruction for the apostles (v. 20)

"It is not ye that speak, but the Spirit of your Father who speaketh in you."

(1) The promise of divine inspiration

The apostles wouldn't be speaking—God by His Spirit would speak through them. God gave those men the promise of divine inspiration. That promise also applied to Stephen. When he stood before those who were about to stone him, he spoke the Word of God. Paul did the same when he stood before those who brought him to trial. Their testimonies are part of Scripture.

(2) The implication of biblical inerrancy

Since God gave the apostles the words to speak when they were brought before the councils of men, we can be assured that when those men sat down to pen the Word of God, they could claim the same promise—an implication of far greater importance. Matthew 10:20, one of the clearest texts in the Bible on inspiration, affirms, "It is not

63

ye that speak [Gk., *laloun*, "utter"] but the Spirit of your Father who speaketh in you."

Lenski said, "Without previous thinking, planning, imagining, at the time of their trials in court the apostles will receive directly from God just what to utter. It will come into their minds just as it is needed, and thus they will utter it aloud. . . . The apostles, indeed, make utterance, and yet they do not, for their act is due to the Holy Spirit, so that most properly he is the one who does this uttering. Everything that is mechanical, magical, unpsychological is shut out. . . . The apostles will not be like the demoniacs, their organs of speech and their very wills being violated by a demon. Absolutely the contrary: mind, heart, will operate freely, consciously, in joyful, trustful dependence on the Spirit's giving, who enables them to find just what to say and how to say it down to the last word, with no mistake or even a wrong word due to faulty memory or disturbed emotions occurring. This, of course, is Inspiration, Verbal Inspiration" (p. 402).

5. Be patient (v. 22)

"Ye shall be hated of all men for my name's sake, but he that endureth to the end shall be saved."

The context is persecution, so the text is saying endurance is a hallmark of genuine salvation. It isn't saying that people who can make it through persecution will hold on to their salvation. Those who are saved survive.

a) Romans 2:7—"To them who by patient continuance in well-doing seek for glory and honor and immortality, eternal life." People aren't saved by continuous good deeds, but works do prove the validity of their salvation.

b) Hebrews 3:14—"We are made partakers of Christ, if we hold the beginning of our confidence steadfast unto the end."

c) John 8:31—Jesus said, "If ye continue in my word, then are ye my disciples indeed."

d) 1 John 2:19—"They went out from us, but they were not of us; for if they had been of us, they would no doubt have continued with us."

Sometimes I pray that God will persecute the church because it has the effect of separating wheat from chaff. When persecution begins, the phonies leave. They're not going to die for something they don't believe in.

The Greek word translated "saved" in Matthew 10:22 means "delivered." Go through the persecution, and you will be delivered. First Corinthians 10:13 says, "There hath no temptation taken you but such as is common to man; but God is faithful, who will not permit you to be tempted above that ye are able, but will, with the temptation, also make a way to escape." If you patiently keep the faith, you will endure whatever comes and be delivered.

Paul said, "What shall separate us from the love of Christ? Shall tribulation, or distress, or persecution, or famine, or nakedness, or peril, or sword? As it is written, For thy sake we are killed all the day long; we are accounted as sheep for the slaughter. Nay, in all these things we are more than conquerors through him that loved us. For I am persuaded that neither death, nor life, nor angels, nor principalities, nor powers, nor things present, nor things to come, nor height, nor depth, nor any other creation, shall be able to separate us from the love of God, which is in Christ Jesus, our Lord" (Rom. 8:35-39). Nothing will destroy you. When you are in the midst of persecution, be patient; you will endure to the end and be delivered.

6. Be on the move (v. 23)

"When they persecute you in this city, flee into another; for verily I say unto you, Ye shall not have gone over the cities of Israel, till the Son of man be come."

Keep moving as necessary until Jesus comes again. There is no sense in standing around enduring unnecessary harassment and persistent persecution until someone kills you.

Paul would preach, a riot would start, then he'd leave town and go to another. When a riot broke out there, he went to the next town, and so on. He wasn't going to stay in one place and die—life was too precious; there were too many towns to reach and too much to be done.

The last missionaries will be moving from one place to another when the Son of Man returns. During the Great Tribulation, 144,000 Jewish evangelists will preach all over the land and will keep moving until the Lord comes. When all the cities have been reached, He will come.

We have no right to provoke animosity or destruction. There is too much work to be done and too many places to reach. Life is precious. Every one of us matters to God's kingdom. We have to move to the receptive places and keep moving, knowing that God is with us all the time. In the power of the Spirit He will help us to say the right things and reach the world.

Conclusion

We are sheep among wolves. It was not uncommon in Palestine to hear about a shepherd found dead among the sheep he was trying to defend. But our Shepherd is not dead—He ever lives and is our defender. We have a sense of invincibility because He controls everything. Zechariah 2:8 says, "He that toucheth you toucheth the apple of his eye." God will make all things right in the end. No matter what Satan does, he can't destroy God's sheep.

Focusing on the Facts

1. What is the key word of Matthew 10:17? Why (see p. 55)?

2. How was punishment for a violation of the law or a rabbinical standard carried out in the synagogue (see p. 55)?
3. When did Jewish persecution of Christianity stop (see p. 55)?
4. Where did false religion begin? How was it spread around the world (see p. 56)?
5. What are two possible interpretations of the phrase "for a testimony against them" from Matthew 10:18 (see p. 57)?
6. Why did the Roman government persecute Christians? What accusations did the government bring against Christianity (see pp. 57-58)?
7. Although governments are entities ordained by God to preserve the social structure (Rom. 13), they are also _____ _____ _____ (see p. 58).
8. According to Romans 1:24-26, why would family members persecute their own Christian relatives (see p. 59)?
9. Why are Christians to be "wise as serpents" (Matt. 10:16; pp. 60-61)?
10. What is the meaning of the phrase "harmless as doves"? What does the dove symbolize (Matt. 10:16; p. 61)?
11. What do Christians need to beware of (Matt. 10:17; p. 62)?
12. Why were the disciples not to be anxious when they were brought before councils? Explain (Matt. 10:19; pp. 62-63).
13. According to Matthew 10:20, what did Jesus promise to give the apostles? What is the implication of that promise? Explain (see p. 63).
14. What is a hallmark of genuine salvation? Support your answer with Scripture (Matt. 10:22; p. 64).
15. What effect does persecution have on the church (see p. 65)?
16. Why is there no persecution that can destroy Christians (Rom. 8:35-39; p. 65)?
17. Why did Jesus tell the apostles to keep moving to different places when facing incessant persecution (see pp. 65-66)?

Pondering the Principles

1. To what extent have you experienced persecution from the government or your family? Give examples of each occasion. What has God taught you through each situation? As a result of this lesson, determine how you will prepare for any future persecution from those sources. What must be manifested in your life before anyone will bother to persecute you?

2. Review the six responses of the sheep (see pp. 60-66). When you were persecuted, how did you respond? On a scale of 1 to 10, rate the effectiveness of your wisdom, purity, watchfulness, calmness, patience, and willingness to move. What are your strengths? What are your weaknesses? If future persecution should come your way, what must you do to shore up the responses you are weak in?

5
Christlikeness: The Goal of Discipleship

Outline

Introduction
A. The Responsibility of Leadership
  1. A commitment to God's calling
  2. A commitment to God's will
  3. A commitment to seek disciples
  4. A commitment to follow Christ
  5. A commitment to learn and teach the essentials
B. The Response of Past Disciples
  1. Florence Nightingale
  2. Jim Elliot
  3. Jonathan Edwards

Lesson
  I. A Disciple Is a Follower of Christ (v. 24)
    A. He Claims a Relationship
    B. He Counts the Cost
 II. A Disciple Is Treated Like Christ (v. 24)
    A. Because He Is Associated with His Teacher
      1. A student/teacher relationship
      2. A slave/master relationship
    B. Because He Acts Like His Teacher
III. A Disciple Is Content to Be Like Christ (v. 25)

Conclusion

Introduction

Matthew 10:24-25 says, "The disciple is not above his teacher, nor the servant above his lord. It is enough for the disciple that he be like his teacher, and the servant like his lord. If they have called the master of the house Beelzebub, how much more shall they call them of his household?"

That reflects on the fundamental responsibility of the church as stated by our Lord Jesus Christ: "Go . . . and make disciples of all the nations, baptizing them . . . [and] teaching them to observe all that I commanded you" (Matt. 28:19-20, NASB). Matthew 10 contains Jesus' instructions on what it means to be His disciple.

The Greek word translated "disciple" (*mathētēs*) means "learner." Jesus taught a group of twelve disciples. He helped them to mature spiritually so that they could teach others and advance the kingdom.

We are involved in that process. The commission of the church involves more than leading people to Jesus Christ. We're to equip "the saints for the work of the ministry" (Eph. 4:12). The church is to produce mature disciples who can in turn produce others.

A. The Responsibility of Leadership

Producing mature disciples was the Lord's task when He was on earth, and was also the task of the apostles. In fact, the apostle Paul said repeatedly that his great desire was to bring the saints to maturity (1 Cor. 14:20; Eph. 4:13; Col. 4:12). It is the task of all who are called to Christian leadership.

1. A commitment to God's calling

I know God has called me to teach the Word to help mature the saints. I am accountable to fulfill that calling to the extent possible in the power of the Holy Spirit. That means I must be committed to fighting my weaknesses so that the task God has given me may be accomplished.

70

Are You Tuned In?

One question Christian leaders face is whether people listen when they are taught. The Lord Jesus Christ faced that problem. He knew what His task was and how to communicate the truth, but He sought hearts open to receive it.

Teaching God's truth is like a radio program—it's one thing to broadcast and another to have an attentive audience. For preaching and teaching to be effective, someone has to be tuned in to the message. The "Grace to You" broadcast goes out all over the world, but of all those who could listen to it, relatively few take advantage of their opportunity to tune in. All too often that's how it is in the church—a lot of broadcasting is going on, but only a few are tuned in.

2. A commitment to God's will

   The leadership in a church must be committed to doing God's will as revealed in the Bible. That should be a commitment not only of the leadership, but also of the flock. Often the reason that kind of commitment is lacking is that the church doesn't understand what it means to be a Christian or a disciple of Jesus Christ.

3. A commitment to seek disciples

   When Jesus called His disciples, He carefully warned them about what they would face. He discouraged half-hearted people from following Him. He used metaphors such as the narrow gate and the narrow way (Matt. 7:13-14) to illustrate the separation between Himself and those who weren't willing to pay the price of commitment to Him. The challenge to the Lord, His apostles, and ministers today is the same: find people who are willing and eager to respond obediently to God's Word, no matter what the price.

4. A commitment to follow Christ

   True discipleship means that a person commits himself to follow Jesus Christ for life. You may have wondered

71

about the necessity of dedication in the Christian walk. Many have gone to a church and watched someone give an altar call where people go to the front of the church and dedicate, rededicate, consecrate, reconsecrate, commit, or recommit their lives to Christ. The essence of dedication, commitment, or consecration to Christ—to be set apart or sanctified in Him—is what Matthew 10:24-42 is all about.

5. A commitment to learn and teach the essentials

Jesus' teachings on discipleship in Matthew 10:24-42 are essential truths of the faith. We know that because our Lord repeated them many times (e.g., Matt. 16:24-25; Luke 14:26-35; John 8:31; 12:26; 15:1–16:4). Good Bible teachers recognize certain essential truths in Scripture. Through study and experience such teachers find concise and effective ways to communicate those basics so that they are understandable. Once in a while you may hear the same terminology, illustrations, concepts, and expressions used because they have been tested for effectiveness.

Redaction Criticism: No Repetition Allowed

So-called "redaction critics" believe Matthew wasn't a writer who recorded what Jesus actually said to His disciples but an editor who sorted and condensed Jesus' teachings, which were given at different times. They essentially accuse him of misrepresenting the material in Matthew 10 as one speech by the Lord Jesus Christ.

One of their reasons is that the material is found elsewhere in the gospels. Redaction critics are unwilling to allow for repetition as a valid teaching method employed by Jesus. But it is reasonable to conclude that like any other teacher, Jesus taught the same truths in different places and circumstances. Although He varied His terminology according to the situation, He taught the same essential principles.

Redaction criticism destroys the integrity of Matthew, taints the authority of Jesus' recorded teachings, and denies that Jesus had the right to repeat Himself as occasion warranted. Yet Scripture speaks of learning "precept upon precept; line upon line" (Isa. 28:10). Jesus taught the essential truths of the gospel many times, and one of His favorite subjects was discipleship.

B. The Response of Past Disciples

Those who properly respond to the truths of Matthew 10:24-42 are the kind of people God uses to change the course of history.

1. Florence Nightingale

Florence Nightingale, nineteenth-century nursing pioneer, wrote in her diary, "To-day I am 30—the age Christ began His mission. Now no more childish things. . . . Now Lord let me think only of Thy will" (Cecil Woodham-Smith, *Florence Nightingale* [N.Y.: McGraw-Hill, 1951], p. 53). She had the reputation of keeping nothing back from God. Not holding back is what Matthew 10 is all about.

2. Jim Elliot

Jim Elliot, a missionary to the Auca Indians in Ecuador, wrote in his diary, "God, I pray Thee, light these idle sticks of my life and may I burn up for Thee. Consume my life, my God, for it is Thine. I seek not a long life but a full one, like You, Lord Jesus" (Elisabeth Elliot, *Shadow of the Almighty* [N.Y.: Harper & Row, 1958], p. 55). That's exactly what he got—in the flower of his youth an Auca Indian fatally speared him.

3. Jonathan Edwards

God mightily used the eighteenth-century American pastor and theologian Jonathan Edwards because he was willing to pay the price of true discipleship. In his memoirs he wrote, "I have been before God, and have given myself, all that I am and have, to God; so that I am not, in any respect, my own. I can challenge no right in this understanding, this will, these affections, which are in me. Neither have I any right to this body, or any of its members—no right to this tongue, these hands, these feet; no right to these senses, these eyes, these ears, this smell, or this taste. I have given myself clear away, and have not retained any thing as my own. . . .

"I pray God, for the sake of Christ, to look upon it as a self-dedication, and to receive me now as entirely his own, and to deal with me, in all respects, as such, whether he afflicts me or prospers me, or whatever he pleases to do with me, who am his.

"Now, henceforth, I am not to act, in any respect, as my own—I shall act as my own, if I ever make use of any of my powers to do any thing that is not to the glory of God, and do not make the glorifying of him my whole and entire business:—if I murmur in the least at affliction; if I grieve at the prosperity of others; if I am in any way uncharitable; if I am angry because injuries; if I revenge them; if I do any thing purely to please myself, or avoid any thing for the sake of my own ease; if I omit any thing because it is great self-denial; if I trust to myself; if I take any of the praise of the good that I do, or that God doth by me; or if I am in any way proud" (*The Works of Jonathan Edwards*, vol. 1 [Edinburgh: Banner of Truth Trust, 1974], p. xxv). Edwards was a man who belonged absolutely to God.

Lesson

I. A DISCIPLE IS A FOLLOWER OF CHRIST (v. 24)

"The disciple is not above his teacher, nor the servant above his lord."

A. He Claims a Relationship

The twelve apostles were the primary audience for Jesus' teaching in Matthew 10. They were to be sent out for a short time of ministry to prepare them for final commissioning after the resurrection. But in verse 23 Jesus refers to those who would minister "till the son of man [returns]"— until the second coming. So the Lord's teaching telescopes to encompass all who would follow Him in the future. That broad audience is also addressed in Matthew 10:24-42.

Jesus' use of the word "disciple" in verse 24 emphasizes the broad scope of His audience. The twelve apostles had been named and trained prior to verse 24 (vv. 1-15). But after verse 24 Christ used the terms "disciple" (vv. 24-25, 42), "servant" (vv. 24-25), "whosoever" (vv. 33, 42), and "he that" (vv. 37-41) to emphasize the learning process that applies to any individual who claims to have a relationship with Him.

B. He Counts the Cost

Jesus broadened the scope of His audience as He explained what it meant to be His disciple. He made a point of presenting the cost of discipleship up front. We don't do anyone a favor by trying to get him or her to "make a decision" for Christ without explaining what belonging to Him will cost. Many false believers come into the church because they are never presented with the cost of discipleship.

1. John 6:53-66—"Except ye eat the flesh of the Son of man, and drink his blood, ye have no life in you. . . . From that time many of his disciples went back, and walked no more with him." Jesus meant that His followers must accept His sacrifice on their behalf for salvation, but many would not accept that.

2. Matthew 8:19-20—"A certain scribe came, and said unto him, Master, I will follow thee wherever thou goest. And Jesus saith unto him, The foxes have holes, and the birds of the air have nests, but the Son of man hath not where to lay his head." The text implies that in response the man left—he apparently wasn't willing to be deprived of earthly comforts.

3. Matthew 8:21-22—"Another of his disciples said unto him, Lord, permit me first to go and bury my father. But Jesus said unto him, Follow me, and let the dead bury their dead." That man wanted to wait until his father died, so he could receive his inheritance. Evidently that disciple also stopped following Jesus.

75

4. Luke 9:61-62—"Another also said, Lord, I will follow thee; but let me first go bid them farewell, who are at home at my house. And Jesus said unto him, No man, having put his hand to the plough, and looking back, is fit for the kingdom of God." Jesus meant that discipleship would sever that man's family ties.

The way that leads to eternal life is narrow (Matt. 7:13-14). There is a cost. That's the way the Lord has always presented discipleship.

Theological Hash?

Matthew's record of Jesus' teaching is so clear and logical that it's hard to understand why redaction critics say it is but a hodgepodge of unassociated sayings. They say the same about the Sermon on the Mount. Supposedly Matthew took various sayings of Jesus and made it look as if Jesus spoke it all at one time—a theological hash without a logical pattern. But that approach fails to recognize the logical flow and genius of Jesus' teaching as recorded by Matthew. Matthew 10 clearly tells us how to minister (vv. 5-15), what kind of reactions to expect (vv. 18-23), and the cost of discipleship (vv. 24-42). That's not theological hash; it's a logical progression.

II. A DISCIPLE IS TREATED LIKE CHRIST (v. 24)

"The disciple is not above his teacher, nor the servant above his lord."

A. Because He Is Associated with His Teacher

By the time Jesus reached verse 24 in His teaching, the apostles had been told they would be like sheep among wolves (v. 16), scourged (v. 17), dragged before pagan courts (v. 18), persecuted by their own families (v. 21), hated by all (v. 22), and forced to run from city to city (v. 23). In verse 24 Jesus begins His teaching on the cost of discipleship with two examples: "a disciple is not above his teacher, nor a slave above his master" (NASB). Jesus' disciples were not to expect to be treated differently. That's an axiomatic part of a relationship to Christ (cf. Luke 6:40).

76

1. A student/teacher relationship

   Students learn what their teachers tell them. That's a role they adopt by choice. Since they place themselves under their teacher's instruction, they obviously can't be above their teacher.

2. A slave/master relationship

   A slave is chosen or bought by his master. He has no choice—he must obey. The master is always above his slave.

Subservience to Christ as Lord is the point of Jesus' examples. Students obey according to their choice of position and slaves obey by the compulsion of their position. We choose to be disciples and learn at the feet of Jesus, but He sovereignly chose us first to be His slaves.

B. Because He Acts Like His Teacher

   1. Luke 6:40—"A pupil [disciple] is not above his teacher; but everyone, after he has been fully trained, will be like his teacher" (NASB).

   2. 1 John 2:6—"He that saith he abideth in him ought himself also so to walk, even as he walked."

   3. Colossians 3:16—"Let the word of Christ dwell in you richly." We are to be dominated by Christ's Word so we become like Him.

   4. Matthew 10:27—Jesus said, "What I tell you in darkness, that speak in light." We say what He said. We have no other message than Christ's Word.

   5. 1 John 3:2—"When [Christ] shall appear, we shall be like him; for we shall see him as he is."

The goal of all Christian life is to conform to Christ's likeness. The result is that the world will treat Christians as it treated Christ. The disciples of a persecuted teacher will also be persecuted. A person who is increasingly like

Christ will be treated increasingly like He was. In Matthew 10:24 Jesus clearly tells us that if we aren't willing to come to Him on those terms, we are not part of Him.

III. A DISCIPLE IS CONTENT TO BE LIKE CHRIST (v. 25)

"It is enough for the disciple that he be like his teacher, and the servant like his lord. If they have called the master of the house Beelzebub, how much more shall they call them of his household?"

A true disciple is content to be like his teacher, just as an obedient slave is content to be like his lord. The Greek word translated "enough" (*arketos*) means "sufficient." Disciples of Christ don't try to escape what their Lord couldn't escape. It is sufficient for them to live as He lived and be treated as He was.

Paul's prayer was that he would truly know Christ and the fellowship of His sufferings (Phil. 3:10). He didn't ask for fame, acceptance, or the world's love. Rather he knew that to be successful in pursuing Christ involves knowing and experiencing what He experienced.

A number of times Jesus was accused of working for the devil (cf. Matt. 9:34; 12:24). Since He ("the master of the house") was called the devil ("Beelzebub"), His disciples ("them of his household") could certainly expect to be called the same thing.

Conclusion

Believers must be willing to pay the cost of conforming to Christ, which is the goal of discipleship. That means the followers of Christ will be treated like their master. Our Lord was clear about that:

A. John 13:16—"The servant is not greater than his lord; neither he that is sent greater than he that sent him."

B. John 15:18-21—"If the world hate you, ye know that it hated me before it hated you. If ye were of the world, the world would love its own; but because ye are not of the world, but I have chosen you out of the world, therefore

78

the world hateth you. Remember the word that I said unto you, The servant is not greater than his lord. If they have persecuted me, they will also persecute you; if they have kept my saying, they will keep yours also. But all these things will they do unto you for my name's sake, because they know not him that sent me."

C. John 16:2—"The time cometh, that whosoever killeth you will think that he doeth God service."

In spite of the world's treatment, God moves the hearts of people to redeem them. Many people become Christians because of what they see in the life of a believer. Joy, peace, freedom from guilt, a sense of forgiveness, and the hope of eternal life are all attractive to those God calls to Himself, while at the same time they are distasteful to a world that hates Christ. That's the price of discipleship.

Focusing on the Facts

1. What is the fundamental responsibility of the church (Matt. 28:19-20; see p. 70)?
2. Producing mature _____ was the Lord's task when He was on earth (see p. 70).
3. What does the Greek word translated "disciple" (*mathētēs*) mean (see p. 70)?
4. According to Ephesians 4:12, what process takes place in the church (see p. 70)?
5. What is the task of all who are called to Christian leadership (see p. 70)?
6. How is teaching God's truth like a radio program? What does that mean (see p. 71)?
7. What kinds of commitment are leaders in the church called to? Summarize each kind (see pp. 71-72).
8. What does redaction criticism claim (see p. 72)?
9. What characterizes those who properly respond to the truths of Matthew 10:24-42 (see pp. 73-74)?
10. Who is the primary audience for Jesus' teaching in Matthew 10 (see p. 74)?
11. Is Christ's teaching in Matthew 10:24-42 directed to a broad or narrow audience? Explain (see pp. 74-75).

12. Many false believers come into the church because they were never presented with the _____ of discipleship (see p. 75).
13. The way that leads to _____ _____ is narrow (see p. 76).
14. Discuss the progression of Jesus' teaching in Matthew 10 (see p. 76).
15. What will association with Christ result in (see p. 76)?
16. The goal of Christian life is conformity to _____ _____ (see p. 77).
17. What will happen to a person who is increasingly like Christ (see pp. 77-78)?
18. What is a true disciple content to be? Explain (see p. 78).
19. What did the pursuit of Christ mean to Paul (see p. 78)?
20. What did Jesus say His disciples could expect to be called? Why (Matt. 10:25; see p. 78)?

Pondering the Principles

1. The leadership of the church is to be committed to God's call, God's will, seeking disciples, and teaching the essentials of the faith. But such commitments can be fulfilled with joy only when one's heart is transformed. English hymnwriter Isaac Watts, writing to Christian ministers, said, "Call your own soul often to account; examine the temper, the frame, and the motions of your heart with all holy severity, so that the evidences of your faith in Jesus, and your repentance for sin, and your conversion to God, be many and fair, be strong and unquestionable; that you may walk on with courage and joyful hope toward heaven, and lead on the flock of Christ thither with holy assurance and joy" (cited in *The Christian Ministry; or Excitement and Direction in Ministerial Duties, Extracted from Various Authors*, edited by William Innes [Edinburgh: Waugh and Innes, 1824], pp. 92-93). If you are in Christian leadership, are you constantly making sure of your own transformation as you seek transformation in others?

2. American evangelist Vance Havner said, "Christianity is not a happiness cult; it is not a success cult. At heart it is the process by which God makes saints out of sinners. We are predestinated to be conformed to the image of God's Son. We are not on a glorified picnic, a sanctified hayride. We are afflicted nowadays

with a cheap Christianity, a kind of religious popcorn diet—no cross, no discipline! We receive the Word with joy, but we have no root nor depth and are soon offended. There are too many religious hoboes trying to go to heaven as cheaply as possible, with just enough prayer, Bible reading, and service to get by. Such lives will go up in smoke at the judgment" (*Why Not Just Be Christians?* [Old Tappan, N.J.: Revell, 1964), pp. 28-29). Are you seeking worldly happiness or God's glory?

6
The Hallmarks of Discipleship—Part 1

Outline

Introduction

Review

Lesson
I. A Disciple Does Not Fear the World (vv. 26-31)
   A. He Knows He Will Be Vindicated (v. 26)
      1. The reward
      2. The revelation
   B. He Fears God More than Man (vv. 27-28)
      1. He keeps nothing secret
         a) By telling all
         b) By adding nothing
         c) By making public proclamation
         d) By paying the price
      2. He keeps things in perspective
         a) Persecution by family
         b) The persecution of Paul
         c) The persecution of Latimer
         d) The persecution of early Christians
         e) Persecution during the Dark Ages
         f) Persecution in China
         g) Persecution in Africa
   C. He Knows He Is Valued by God (vv. 29-31)
      1. God's interest
      2. God's care

Conclusion

Introduction

Matthew's purpose in writing was to affirm that Christ is King. He knew that mankind is prone to raise up other monarchs who compete with Christ. When a person becomes a Christian, he submits willingly to Jesus Christ as Lord, Master, and King. He gives himself to Christ's sovereignty, turning away from the petty monarchs in his past. In Matthew 10:24-42 we find our Lord's instructions to those committed to His sovereignty.

Review

Christ's teaching embraces all who claim a relationship with Him—not just a special few. If we claim a relationship to Christ, we are to follow and learn from Him. As a result we will be like Him. We will cling to His values and submit to His authority.

The world stooped low enough to label Christ as the devil, and it won't hesitate to do the same to us. In Matthew 10:25 Jesus uses the analogy of a master of a house—a person with dignity, authority, honor, and wealth. If people dare to malign the master, they will certainly not hesitate to speak evil against those who belong to his household.

However, true disciples are content to be like Christ. That is their goal, so they are willing to pay the cost of discipleship.

Lesson

True disciples are characterized by certain hallmarks.

I. A DISCIPLE DOES NOT FEAR THE WORLD (vv. 26-31)

In Matthew 10 Jesus instructs His disciples not to fear the world (vv. 26, 28, 31), but fear would be the natural response to the warnings given in verses 16-23. Proverbs 29:25 explains, "The fear of man bringeth a snare; but whoso putteth his trust in the Lord shall be safe." The fear of man strangles effective evangelism. Because we don't want to experience difficulty, disrespect, or persecution, we often hold back from telling the good news of Jesus Christ.

Too often Christians are caught up in self-preservation. Jesus warned that persecution would occur, but He wanted His disciples to be bold in the midst of it. First John 2:15 says, "Love not the world, neither the things that are in the world. If any man love the world, the love of the Father is not in him." A person who is afraid of the world, disinterested in witnessing for Christ, and unwilling to pay the price of discipleship is unlikely to be a real Christian. His priorities are wrong. When the pressure is on, such people bail out: "They went out from us, but they were not of us" (1 John 2:19). Those who remain faithful to Christ under pressure give evidence of being true disciples.

Fear and the Frozen River

Christ often reminded His disciples not to be afraid: "Fear not, little flock; for it is your Father's good pleasure to give you the kingdom" (Luke 12:32). Even after His resurrection, Jesus reminded His disciples not to be afraid (Matt. 28:10; Luke 24:38; John 20:19-23). Christians constantly need to be encouraged to avoid fear. We need to get away from the church and our Bible studies enough to proclaim God's Word to a world that doesn't know Jesus Christ. We need to avoid being like the Arctic River: frozen over at the mouth.

A. He Knows He Will Be Vindicated (v. 26)

"Fear them not, therefore; for there is nothing covered that shall not be revealed; and hidden, that shall not be known."

"Therefore" looks back to what Jesus had previously said—that since He experienced persecution in the world, they should expect the same. Nevertheless, they were not to be afraid because "there is nothing covered that shall not be revealed; and hidden, that shall not be known" (v. 26).

The truth about everything will one day be made known. Now Christians are often looked down on as anti-intellectual outcasts and are persecuted. The worldly are successful, and the wicked prosper. Yet that will change—the truth will become clear.

God will reveal those who are truly successful and vindicate those who are His. What is now hidden will be revealed when God exercises vengeance upon those who do not know Him. Jesus wanted His disciples to have an eternal perspective—one that would enable them to avoid fear.

1. The reward

   Scripture assures believers of their reward.

   a) Revelation 22:12—Jesus said, "Behold, I come quickly, and my reward is with me, to give every man according as his work shall be."

   b) 2 Corinthians 5:10—"We must all appear before the judgment seat of Christ, that everyone may receive the things done in his body, according to that he hath done, whether it be good or bad."

   c) 1 Corinthians 4:5—"Judge nothing . . . until the Lord come, who both will bring to light the hidden things of darkness, and will make manifest the counsels of the hearts; and then shall every man have praise of God."

   d) Revelation 2:10—Jesus said, "Be thou faithful unto death, and I will give thee a crown of life."

   e) 2 Timothy 4:8—Paul said assuredly, "There is laid up for me a crown of righteousness, which the Lord, the righteous judge, shall give me at that day."

   f) 1 Corinthians 9:25—The worldly strive "to obtain a corruptible crown, but we, an incorruptible [one]."

   g) 1 Thessalonians 2:19—Paul said of the Thessalonians, "What is our hope, or joy, or crown of rejoicing? Are not even ye in the presence of our Lord Jesus Christ at his coming?"

Those who have an eternal perspective don't worry about being popular or appearing wise and noble in this life. That perspective enables any disciple to confront society with the claims of Christ while anticipating reward in eternity.

2. The revelation

We need to live for the future. Only then will we know who were hypocrites and who were heroes. Many Christians trade momentary popularity for an eternal reward.

a) Luke 12:1-2—Jesus said to His disciples, "Beware of the leaven of the Pharisees, which is hypocrisy. For there is nothing covered, that shall not be revealed; neither hidden, that shall not be known." Here the phrase used in Matthew 10:26 refers to the unmasking of hypocrites—those who hide the truth about themselves.

b) Luke 8:16-17—"No man, when he hath lighted a lamp, covereth it with a vessel, or putteth it under a bed, but setteth it on a lampstand, that they who enter in may see the light. For nothing is secret, that shall not be made manifest; neither any thing hidden, that shall not be known and come to light."

c) 1 Corinthians 3:12-13—"If any man build upon this foundation gold, silver, precious stones, wood, hay, stubble—every man's work shall be made manifest; for the day shall declare it, because it shall be revealed by fire; and the fire shall test every man's work of what sort it is."

d) Ecclesiastes 11:9—"Rejoice, O young man, in thy youth, and let thy heart cheer thee in the days of thy youth, and walk in the ways of thine heart, and in the sight of thine eyes; but know thou, that for all these things God will bring thee into judgment."

e) Ecclesiastes 12:13-14—"Fear God, and keep his commandments; for this is the whole duty of man. For God shall bring every work into judgment, with every secret thing, whether it be good, or whether it be evil."

Someday God will expose the entire record of our lives. Many who looked like winners in this life will be revealed as eternal losers, whereas others who were persecuted for their faith and viewed as losers will be revealed as eternal winners.

John Calvin and another minister were banished from Geneva after preaching God's truth. When Calvin was notified, he said, "If we had served men, we should have been ill rewarded. But we serve a great Master who will recompense us" (Jean Moura and Paul Lovet, *Calvin: A Modern Biography* [Garden City, N.Y.: Doubleday, 1932], p. 158).

B. He Fears God More than Man (vv. 27-28)

"What I tell you in darkness, that speak in light; and what ye hear in the ear, that proclaim upon the housetops. And fear not them who kill the body, but are not able to kill the soul; but rather fear him who is able to destroy both soul and body in hell."

A person who truly worships and fears God does not fear man.

1. He keeps nothing secret

There are no secrets in Christianity. We are to present the message of the gospel as we have received it.

At the time Jesus taught, the rabbis would train their pupils by standing beside them and speaking privately into their ears. Then the young men would repeat what they had been told. The Lord used that picture to show how the disciples were to speak openly what they had been told privately.

a) By telling all

When Jesus said, "What I tell you in darkness, that speak in light; and what ye hear in the ear, that proclaim upon the housetops" (v. 27), He set no restrictions on proclaiming what He taught them. We are to hold back nothing our Lord has chosen to reveal.

Often Christians hold back God's truth for fear of alienating non-Christians. Much of today's evangelism consists of questions such as, "Would you like to be happy?" "Would you like to have all your problems solved and live in heaven forever?" "Would you like to experience true love?" Apparently those who ask such questions think they will make Jesus so desirable that unsaved people will end up asking, "Where do I sign?"

If you were to approach someone you work with and lovingly say, "My friend, do you know you are in danger of burning in hell forever if you don't receive salvation through Jesus Christ?" you would probably get persecuted. Because that kind of message offends people, many Christians refrain from disclosing crucial spiritual truths.

b) By adding nothing

Verse 27 means we are to tell nothing less than the whole truth but also nothing more. That means first getting alone with God and poring over His Word. Only from that secret place of study and prayer may we speak God's Word to others. When we add to the message of God's Word, we confuse people about the truth.

c) By making public proclamation

In the days of Christ's ministry on earth, announcements were commonly made from housetops. Houses had flat roofs with short walls around the edges that served as patios. People often slept, ate, and entertained on their roofs. Making an announcement only required that a person stand on his roof and shout. A high roof would be an advantage, and many people were likely to hear such an announcement because people tended to be outside. Also there were no cars, TVs, or stereos to drown out the sound. Christ wanted His disciples to be as public as possible with the gospel.

Rabbis sometimes taught from housetops, and religious officials announced religious holidays by blowing a trumpet from a housetop. That is similar to the minarets used today in the Moslem world by which Muslims are called to prayer. First-century Jewish historian Josephus wrote about a time when he tried to calm an angry mob by addressing the people from the roof of his house (*Wars of the Jews*, 2.21.5). Housetops were the common public forum of Jesus' day. Today we're to use whatever common public forums are available to us to proclaim the gospel.

d) By paying the price

There is a price to pay for telling the entire gospel. Acts 21:10-11 records how the prophet Agabus warned Paul that he would be imprisoned for preaching the gospel in Jerusalem. The text then records Paul's resolution to complete his ministry in the face of persecution. Paul's example shows us that the gospel is never to be kept secret and that there is a price to pay for publicly proclaiming it.

2. He keeps things in perspective

Jesus said, "Fear not them who kill the body, but are not able to kill the soul; but rather fear him who is able to destroy both soul and body in hell" (Matt. 10:28). Man can kill only the body, not the soul. The worst he can do is only temporal. Paul said, "For to me to live is Christ, and to die is gain" (Phil. 1:21).

However, God is able to destroy both soul and body in hell forever. Hell is where Satan himself will be subjected to continual persecution. Only God has the keys to death and hell (Rev. 1:18), so only God should be feared. Man's power is puny beside God's. Matthew was not threatening Christians with hell. He was pointing out that all mankind should fear the One who determines the destiny of both soul and body, not those who can determine merely when and how to kill the body.

Whether we fear God is revealed by how we react to opportunities to share the gospel that will clearly result in persecution.

a) Persecution by family

When we fail to communicate the gospel to our family members because we know they will be angry, we show that we fear man more than God. If we truly fear God and revere His infinite holiness and majesty, worshiping Him as He ought to be worshiped, we will speak on His behalf regardless of any threat that stands in our way.

Go to Hell to Get Away from It All?

Some people think the destruction in hell described in Scripture means total annihilation. But that is not what the Greek word translated "destroy" in Matthew 10:28 means. It's the ongoing destruction spoken of in 2 Thessalonians 1:8-9: "On them that know not God, and that obey not the gospel of our Lord Jesus Christ, who shall be punished with everlasting destruction from the presence of the Lord."

The destruction of hell is continual and forever. In Matthew 10:28 the Greek word translated "hell" is *Gehenna*. It was the name of the city dump in the Valley of Hinnom outside of Jerusalem. Jesus used it to illustrate the terrible nature of hell because in that dump worms continually fed upon the garbage, and fires were perpetually lit to burn the trash.

In hell the unsaved will be consumed in their resurrection bodies forever. People often wonder if there is literal fire in hell. Since the unsaved are resurrected to eternal life with literal bodies (Rev. 20:11-15), it follows that the fire in hell is literal and eternal. We don't know exactly what kind of fire it will be, but it will be terrible! People must be warned about what they face apart from Christ!

91

b) The persecution of Paul

Paul obeyed God's call to preach the gospel because he feared God. He reverenced God so deeply that he could never say no to God in order to say yes to men. Those who truly venerate God do not fear men because they are focused on obeying God and fearing Him alone. I'd rather fall into the hands of angry men than the hands of an angry God.

c) The persecution of Latimer

William Barclay tells us that sixteenth-century English minister Hugh Latimer "was preaching when Henry the king [Henry VIII] was present. He knew that he was about to say something which the king would not relish. So in the pulpit he soliloquised aloud with himself. 'Latimer! Latimer! Latimer!' he said, 'be careful what you say. Henry the king is here.' Then he paused, and . . . said, 'Latimer! Latimer! Latimer! Be careful what you say. The King of king's is here'" (*The Gospel of Matthew*, vol. 1 [Philadelphia: Westminster, 1958], p. 397; cf. *Foxe's Book of Martyrs* [Grand Rapids: Baker, 1978], pp. 273-74). The king didn't like what he heard, and Latimer was eventually burned at the stake.

d) The persecution of early Christians

During the persecutions endured by the church in its early years, many Christians hid in underground caverns in Rome and outlying areas. They dug many miles of catacombs and buried their dead there for a period of nearly 300 years. Archaeologists estimate that as many as four million Christians were buried in those catacombs.

e) Persecution during the Dark Ages

It is estimated that millions of Christians died for their faith during the Dark Ages.

f) Persecution in China

Countless numbers of Christians died for their faith when the Communists took over China.

g) Persecution in Africa

Many also died for the name of Christ in the civil wars and rebellions that have taken place in Africa.

The Unbound Soul

Although man can kill the body, he can't touch the soul. The immaterial part of every man and woman exists eternally. Man need not worry about persecution of his material body because it is only bound to this earth. Christians look forward to shedding the old body and being resurrected into a new body. If we are worried about what people do to our physical body, we are too earthbound. We are to have the perspective that present persecution is nothing compared to the vindication that will be ours in eternity.

Jesus' warning in Matthew 10:28 must have been particularly poignant for Judas and those like him. There will always be phonies in the church, and verse 28 serves as a terrible warning that God will destroy them both soul and body in hell forever.

C. He Knows He Is Valued by God (vv. 29-31)

"Are not two sparrows sold for a farthing? And one of them shall not fall on the ground without your Father. But the very hairs of your head are all numbered. Fear not, therefore; ye are of more value than many sparrows."

1. God's interest

The Greek word for "farthing" (*assarion*) is approximately equivalent to a penny. The word translated "sparrows" refers to little birds. Two small birds could be bought for a penny or five birds for two cents (Luke

12:6). Those little birds were bought to be served by the plateful as hors d'oeuvres.

Yet verse 29 affirms that not one of those inexpensive little birds falls to the ground without God's knowing and caring about it. Nothing happens in the most simple and seemingly insignificant life that God doesn't know and care about. And God is the Father of every disciple. He knows all about us and even assigns a number to every hair on our heads, which is about 100,000 for the average person according to the most recent *World Book Encyclopedia*.

2. God's care

The lesson of verses 29-30 is summed up in verse 31: "Fear not, therefore; ye are of more value than many sparrows." The same God who cares for little birds cares for us also and values us much more! We will never get into a situation where God will not care for us and sustain us.

a) Psalm 91:7—"A thousand shall fall at thy side, and ten thousand at thy right hand, but it shall not come near thee." Everything may collapse around us, but we will remain safe because God cares for us.

b) Matthew 6:28-30—"Consider the lilies of the field. . . . If God so clothe the grass of the field . . . shall he not much more clothe you, O ye of little faith?"

We're often fearful that we will lose our reputation or job, or that we'll be injured. But Jesus said not to fear because we are of great worth. God will take care of us.

Conclusion

Matthew 10:26-31 explains how we should react to being treated as our Lord was. We should not be afraid because we'll be vindicated in the end with an eternal reward. We should maintain a proper perspective by fearing God not man. And we should also keep in mind the fact that God highly values us. That should diminish our fears regarding how others react to us.

Focusing on the Facts

1. The fear of man strangles effective _____ (see p. 84).
2. What reasons often keep us from telling the good news of Jesus Christ (see pp. 84-85)?
3. Often Christians are caught up in _____ _____ (see p. 85).
4. Who gives the best evidence of being true disciples of Christ (see p. 85)?
5. What kind of perspective did Jesus want His disciples to have? Why (see p. 86)?
6. A person who truly worships and fears God does not fear _____ (see p. 88).
7. What kind of restrictions did Jesus set on the contents of the message His disciples were to pass on (see pp. 88-89)?
8. Why do Christians often hold back God's truth? What kind of gospel presentation does that result in (see p. 89)?
9. Christians are to tell nothing less than the whole truth. How are we to avoid adding to the truth (see p. 89)?
10. Where are we to proclaim the gospel today (see p. 90)?
11. Why is God to be feared (Matt. 10:28; see pp. 90-91)?
12. What situation presents us with an opportunity to show whom we fear—man or God (see p. 91)?
13. Is the destruction of hell continual and forever? Explain (see p. 91)?
14. Of the two parts that constitute man, why don't we need to worry about persecution to the material part (see p. 92)?
15. According to Jesus in Matthew 10:31, why shouldn't we be afraid (see p. 94)?

Pondering the Principles

1. Often people fail to commit themselves to Christ because they are not told of God's resources. Salvation appears to them as something that occurs apart from God's power. They assume they will have to pay the cost of discipleship from their own re-

sources and are apt to turn away from Christ. Puritan Thomas Watson wrote, "There is a promise that works for our good, 'I will be with him in trouble' (Psalm 91.15). God does not bring His people into troubles, and leave them there. He will stand by them; He will hold their heads and hearts when they are fainting. And there is another promise, 'He is their strength in the time of trouble' (Psalm 37.39). 'Oh,' says the soul, 'I shall faint in the day of trial.' But God will be the strength of our hearts; He will join His forces with us. Either He will make His hand lighter, or our faith stronger" (*All Things for Good* [Edinburgh: Banner of Truth Trust, 1986 reprint], p. 16). Take comfort that the cost of discipleship is met with God's own resources, which He has given you in Christ.

2. First John 4:18 affirms that "there is no fear in love. But perfect love drives out fear, because fear has to do with punishment. The man who fears is not made perfect in love" (NIV*). Believers have no fear of coming judgment. But godly fear is different. British pastor Charles Haddon Spurgeon said, "There is a holy fear which must not be banished from the church of God. There is a sacred anxiety which puts us to the question, and examines us whether we be in the faith, and it is not to be disdained" (cited in *Spurgeon at His Best*, edited by Tom Carter [Grand Rapids: Baker, 1988], pp. 77-78). Godly fear characterizes those who recognize who God is and desire to please Him. Is that the attitude of your heart?

New International Version.

7
The Hallmarks of Discipleship—Part 2

Outline

Introduction
A. The Passage
B. The Price

Review
I. A Disciple Does Not Fear the World (vv. 26-31)

Lesson
II. A Disciple Confesses Christ Before Others (vv. 32-33)
A. Those Who Confess Christ (v. 32)
1. The reason for their confession
2. The meaning of their confession
3. The motivation for their confession
4. The audience for their confession
5. The source of their confession
6. The necessity of their confession
7. The result of their confession
8. The wonder of their confession
B. Those Who Deny Christ (v. 33)
1. The open rejectors
2. The secret rejectors
a) How they deny Christ
(1) By their silence
(2) By their actions
b) What their punishment is

Conclusion

Introduction

A. The Passage

Matthew 10:24-33 says, "The disciple is not above his teacher, nor the servant above his lord. It is enough for the disciple that he be like his teacher, and the servant like his lord. If they have called the master of the house Beelzebub, how much more shall they call them of his household? Fear them not, therefore; for there is nothing covered that shall not be revealed; and hidden, that shall not be known. What I tell you in darkness, that speak in light; and what ye hear in the ear, that proclaim upon the housetops. And fear not them who kill the body, but are not able to kill the soul; but rather fear him who is able to destroy both soul and body in hell. Are not two sparrows sold for a farthing? And one of them shall not fall on the ground without your Father. But the very hairs of your head are all numbered. Fear not, therefore; ye are of more value than many sparrows. Whosoever, therefore, shall confess me before men, him will I confess also before my Father, who is in heaven. But whosoever shall deny me before men, him will I also deny before my Father, who is in heaven."

B. The Price

In his book *I Love Idi Amin*, Festo Kivengere, a leading evangelical minister in Uganda, describes the history of the church in Uganda. In 1885 "three Christian boys had shed their blood for Christ in Uganda. The king had ordered the arrest of these page boys in an effort to stamp out Christianity. The eldest was fifteen, and the youngest was eleven-year-old Yusufu.

"They held fast their faith and staked their lives on it, though people were weeping and their parents were pleading with them. At the place of execution they sent a message to the king:

"'Tell His Majesty that he has put our bodies in the fire, but we won't be long in the fire. Soon we shall be with Jesus, which is much better. But ask him to repent and change his mind, or he will land in a place of eternal fire and desolation.'

"They sang a song which is now well-loved in Uganda as the 'martyr's song.' One verse says, 'O that I had wings like the angels. I would fly away and be with Jesus!'

"Little Yusufu said, 'Please don't cut off my arms. I will not struggle in the fire that takes me to Jesus!' Forty adults came to Jesus the day the boys died. This was a new kind of life, which fire and torture could not control.

"We have a Memorial near Kampala where these youngsters are remembered as the first Christian martyrs of Uganda.

"By 1887, the end of the first decade of the church, hundreds had died. There were martyrs out of every village that had believers. They were only beginners, they knew little theology, and some could barely read, but they had fallen in love with Jesus Christ. Life had taken on a completely new meaning. The value of living and living eternally had been discovered. They were not hugging their lives, but ready to give them up for Jesus" ([Old Tappan, N.J.: Revell, 1977] p. 11).

The history of the church is marked by those who have been unashamed of Jesus Christ and willing to confess Him before men regardless of the cost. That is what marks a true disciple. It is not knowledge or length of time that defines what a Christian is but a willingness to confess Christ. On the other hand, a denial of Christ before men is the mark of a false disciple. We need to examine ourselves to see whether we are true or false disciples. Whom do we confess or deny?

Review

Matthew 10:24-42 is a grand summation by our Lord of the meaning of discipleship. Some of what He said in Matthew 10:5-23 is directed explicitly to the twelve, but verse 24 begins a series of instructions on the nature of genuine discipleship.

In verses 24-25 Christ shows that the goal of discipleship is to be like Him. A fully mature disciple is like his teacher (Luke 6:40). "He that saith he abideth in him ought himself also so to walk, even as he walked" (1 John 2:6). Though in times of failure our Christlikeness may be less evident, there is a pattern of Christlikeness in the life of every true believer.

William Barclay wrote, "It is told of J. P. Mahaffy, the famous scholar and man of the world from Trinity College, Dublin, that when he was asked if he was a Christian, his answer was: 'Yes, but not offensively so.' He meant that he did not allow his Christianity to interfere with the society he kept and the pleasure he loved" (*The Gospel of Matthew*, vol. 1, rev. ed. [Philadelphia: Westminster, 1975], p. 391). But that's not what Christianity is. Those who follow Jesus Christ become more and more like Him. If that is not true of you, then you may not be a Christian.

Being a disciple of Christ means that you will be treated like Him. Matthew 10:25 shows that since Christ was called Beelzebub, His followers will be called the same. The more you become like Christ the more of a problem you become to the world—just as He was.

The cost of discipleship means there are few who are genuinely saved (Matt. 7:13-14). There are masses of people who identify with Christianity, but you can distinguish the truly saved among them because they confront the world as their Master did and are often treated as He was.

I. A DISCIPLE DOES NOT FEAR THE WORLD (vv. 26-31; see pp. 84-94)

Increasingly we see the battle lines being drawn between good and evil in our world. Western society has lost its Christian moorings—it is now post-Christian. As a result we may see more and more heat applied to the church. Perhaps that will be the best thing—the heat of persecution will blow away the chaff in the church, and we'll know who the real Christians are. We will also be able to recognize the unsaved and reach out to them.

A true disciple will not fear persecution. He knows God is just, fears Him, and realizes he is valuable in His sight. So he is able to confront evil and confidently confess Christ in the midst of persecution.

II. A DISCIPLE CONFESSES CHRIST BEFORE OTHERS (vv. 32-33)

A. Those Who Confess Christ (v. 32)

"Whosoever, therefore, shall confess me before men, him will I confess also before my Father, who is in heaven."

1. The reason for their confession

Jesus used the word "therefore" in verse 32 to indicate that what He was about to say was based on what He had previously said. The promise, power, and protection of God (vv. 26-31) should make a person willing to confess Jesus Christ before men without fear. That kind of confession is a natural response for the true Christian. Correct doctrine naturally produces proper action. Paul said, "I am not ashamed of the gospel of Christ; for it is the power of God unto salvation" (Rom. 1:16). Paul wasn't ashamed because he knew the promise, power, and protection of God.

2. The meaning of their confession

The Greek word translated "confess" (*homologeō*) means "to affirm," "acknowledge," or "agree." In verse 32 it means making a statement of identification, faith, confidence, trust, and belief in Jesus as Lord and living one's life in accordance with that confession. That confession is displayed by what one says (Rom. 10:9) and does (John 14:23; 1 John 2:17).

3. The motivation for their confession

Because God is the ultimate judge of the earth, there is no excuse for shrinking from our duty to confess Christ in times of persecution as well as in times of peace. All true Christians will confess Christ regardless of the consequences.

4. The audience for their confession

Confession of Christ is to take place "before men" (v. 32). That literally means "in front of men." Our confession is to be public—not in some secret place. A person who refuses to publicly confess Christ is not a Christian. Romans 10:10 affirms that "with the mouth confession is made unto salvation."

5. The source of their confession

Confession is not a work of man but of God. Some say that to require open confession of Christ as evidence of true salvation is works-righteousness. But since Scripture affirms that salvation is completely of God (e.g., Eph. 2:8-10) and that Christians must confess Christ verbally (Rom. 10:10), confession must be the work of God.

6. The necessity of their confession

   a) 1 John 4:15—"Whosoever shall confess that Jesus is the Son of God, God dwelleth in him, and he in God." A person who walked down the aisle one time after an evangelistic service and says he believes but doesn't confess Christ publicly is not a genuine disciple.

   b) Revelation 2:13—Jesus said to the church at Pergamum, "I know thy works, and where thou dwellest, even where Satan's throne is; and thou holdest fast my name, and hast not denied my faith, even in those days in which Antipas was my faithful martyr, who was slain among you." True believers will confess Christ even at the risk of death.

   c) 2 Timothy 4:10—Paul said, "Demas hath forsaken me, having loved this present world, and is departed." Demas is an example of what a disciple is not: when things got tough and the heat was on, he left.

We need to examine ourselves. We may find ourselves ashamed to confess Christ before our families or among friends. If that is our attitude, how would we act during severe persecution? We need to be willing to confess Christ in all circumstances.

Does Our True Confession Mean We Will Never Fail?

In the life of every Christian there will be lapses in living up to the high standard to which we are called. And our Lord has promised forgiveness to those who are genuinely His. Peter was a genuine disciple, and he denied his Lord, but his heart was broken because he knew he had failed to live up to the standard set for him (Matt. 26:69-75; Mark 14:66-72; Luke 22:54-62). Paul told Timothy, a young pastor with talents and gifts, not to be ashamed of Christ or of Paul (2 Tim. 1:8). In each situation Peter and Timothy turned away from weakness and failure to confess Christ. True disciples may fail to confess Christ at times, but that certainly won't be the pattern of their lives.

7. The result of their confession

Jesus said, "Whosoever . . . shall confess me before men, him will I confess also before my Father, who is in heaven" (Matt. 10:32). That means on the Day of Judgment Christ will acknowledge that those who had confessed Him are His. He will affirm His loyalty to us just as we now affirm our loyalty to Him. That is the result of true discipleship. The Lord's words probably pierced deep into the heart of Judas Iscariot just as they do to many false disciples today.

8. The wonder of their confession

Imagine the thrill of someday standing before God and having Jesus say, "This one belongs to Me." If we are loyal to confess the Lord Jesus in the midst of any situation, He has pledged to speak our name in the Father's presence. The Lord of the universe has pledged His loyalty to us.

A Pagan Governor's Understanding of True Christians

During the reign of Roman Emperor Trajan (A.D. 98-117), there was a governor in the province of Bithynia named Pliny. In a letter Pliny detailed to Trajan how he treated the Christians within his province. Anonymous informers told Pliny who were Christians. Pliny gave the accused the opportunity to invoke the gods of Rome, offer wine and incense to the image of the emperor, and curse the name of Christ, "none of which things," Pliny said, "any genuine Christian can be induced to do" (*The Letters of the Younger Pliny*, 10.96).

Even a pagan Roman governor understood the cost of discipleship. He understood that even in the midst of torture, true Christians could not be compelled to deny Christ. We often wonder if we could meet that kind of test but are encouraged to know that God gives grace for such situations. But the cost of discipleship means that there are probably significantly fewer real Christians than it would appear.

B. Those Who Deny Christ (v. 33)

"But whosoever shall deny me before men, him will I also deny before my Father, who is in heaven."

1. The open rejectors

Many openly reject, despise, and hate Christ. My son once told me about a street preacher he and his friends had seen. After listening for a time, he realized the man was giving a good, strong presentation of the gospel. A group of people came up to the preacher, stood only inches away from him, and began to curse at him, yell obscenities about Jesus, and mock him. But he kept on preaching. Some will deny Jesus the way those people did.

2. The secret rejectors

If that street preacher had been a false disciple, he would probably have clammed up and run when the hecklers arrived. In fact, he probably wouldn't have been there to begin with. In Matthew 10:33 Jesus is speaking of people in the sphere of Christianity who seem to have the aura of discipleship. They go along with the externals, but when put to the test they deny the Lord.

a) How they deny Christ

(1) By their silence

People often deceive themselves into believing they can be Christians in secret. They don't reach out to others around them, and no one even knows that they claim the name of Christ. But if no one knows a person is a Christian, it is doubtful that he or she is a Christian.

(2) By their actions

Christ can be denied in many ways short of denial before a firing squad. A worldly life-style, for example, denies Christ (James 4:4).

b) What their punishment is

Denial of Christ eventually will result in denial by Christ in eternity. The "I will confess" of verse 32 and "I will deny" of verse 33 are stated in the future tense. They point to final judgment. On that day many will say to Christ, "Lord, Lord, have we not prophesied in thy name? And in thy name cast out demons? And in thy name done many wonderful works?" (Matt. 7:22). But He will say, "I never knew you; depart from me, ye that work iniquity" (v. 23).

In the heart of every godly pastor is the gnawing anxiety that someone in his flock isn't a true believer and will be eternally damned. Certainly the Lord was concerned about Judas in that way. Judas is a classic example of one who pretends to belong but bails out when the going gets tough. What a fearful price he paid for his thirty pieces of silver!

Conclusion

Matthew 25 contains a picture of what the separation of true and false disciples will be like. At the end of the Tribulation the Lord will separate the sheep from the goats. He will set the sheep (those who love and know Him) on His right and the goats (those who don't know Him) on His left. Verse 34 says, "Then shall the King say unto them on his right hand, Come, ye blessed of my Father, inherit the kingdom prepared for you from the foundation of the world." The King will confess them as His own because they confessed Him. How did they do that?

Certainly they did it with their mouths (Rom. 10:9) and before men (Matt. 10:32). But beyond that the King will say, "I was hungry, and ye gave me food; I was thirsty, and ye gave me drink; I was a stranger, and ye took me in; naked, and ye clothed me; I was sick, and ye visited me; I was in prison, and ye came unto me. Then shall the righteous answer him, saying, Lord, when saw we thee hungry, and fed thee? or thirsty, and gave thee drink? When saw we thee a stranger, and took thee in; or naked, and clothed thee? Or when saw we thee sick, or in prison, and came unto thee? And the King shall answer and say unto them, Verily I say unto you, Inasmuch as you've done it unto one of the least of these my brethren, ye have done it unto me" (Matt. 25:35-40).

Those who truly confess Christ in word and deed will demonstrate His love for His own. "If anyone has material possessions and sees his brother in need but has no pity on him, how can the love of God be in him?" (1 John 3:17, NIV). One way of confessing Christ is responding in the way He would respond in any given situation.

Since the goal of discipleship is to be like Christ, we ought to manifest Christlikeness in our relationships. Many people who say they are Christians come to church and endure the service but have no concern for those around them or the lost people of the world. They're not like Christ, and they exhibit no progression toward Christlikeness in their lives.

We all need to inventory our lives and determine whether Christ is working in us. Only those willing to pay the cost of confessing

Christ before others will be confessed by Him before the Father. Those who by life or lip deny Him will be denied by Him. We will have lapses, but when we in brokenness ask the Lord's forgiveness, He forgives us. That's the attitude of a true believer.

Focusing on the Facts

1. What historically has marked a person as a true disciple of Jesus Christ (see p. 99)?
2. What might be the benefits of persecution of the Western church (see p. 100)?
3. Why doesn't a true disciple fear persecution (see p. 100)?
4. _____ _____ naturally produces proper action (see p. 101).
5. What is the particular meaning of the Greek word *homologeō* in Matthew 10:32 (see p. 101)?
6. Confession of Christ is to take place "_____ _____" (Matthew 10:32; see p. 102).
7. Why is it important to recognize that confession is not a work of man but of God (see p. 102)?
8. Does the necessity of confessing Christ mean that if we fail one time to confess Him, we are lost forever? Why or why not (see p. 103)?
9. What is the result of confessing Christ (see p. 103)?
10. Christ's pledge in Matthew 10:32 means the Lord of the universe has pledged His loyalty to _____ (see p. 103).
11. What did Roman governor Pliny say Christians couldn't be compelled to do (see p. 104)?
12. The cost of discipleship means that there are probably _____ _____ real Christians than it would appear (see p. 104).
13. In Matthew 10:33, what kind of people is Jesus referring to (see p. 105)?
14. In what ways can professing Christians deny Christ (see p. 105)?
15. How will those who deny Christ be punished (see p. 105)?
16. How does Matthew 25:35-40 illustrate confession of Christ (see p. 106)?
17. Since the goal of discipleship is to be like Christ, what should we manifest (see p. 106)?

Pondering the Principles

1. Often when the gospel is presented, the high cost of discipleship is never mentioned. But will a faith that does not require
   sacrifice result in true salvation? In the nineteenth century, An-
   glican bishop J. C. Ryle wrote, "I thoroughly approve of offer-
   ing men a full, free, present, immediate salvation in Christ
   Jesus. I thoroughly approve of urging on man the possibility
   and the duty of immediate instantaneous conversion. . . . But I
   do say that these truths ought not to be set before men nakedly,
   singly, and alone. They ought to be told honestly what it is they
   are taking up, if they profess a desire to come out from the
   world and serve Christ. They ought not to be pressed into the
   ranks of Christ's army without being told what the warfare en-
   tails. In a word, they should be told honestly to count the cost"
   (*Holiness: Its Nature, Hindrances, Difficulties, and Roots* [Welwyn,
   England: Evangelical Press, 1979 reprint], p. 73). How ought the
   cost of discipleship impact the way you present the gospel?

2. Matthew 10:24-42 contains a number of demands. We are to
   proclaim the gospel from the housetops (v. 27), confess Christ
   before men (v. 32), value Christ above our families (v. 37), and
   take up the cross and follow Him (v. 38). Does that mean we obtain salvation by our works? Certainly not! Charles Haddon
   Spurgeon said, "Although we are sure that men are not saved
   for the sake of their works, yet we are equally sure that no man
   will be saved without them" (*The New Park Street Pulpit*, vol. 4
   [Grand Rapids: Zondervan, 1963 reprint], p. 245). Works are a
   natural by-product of saving faith. Consider what the works of
   your life demonstrate about what you believe.

8
The Hallmarks of Discipleship—Part 3

Outline

Introduction
A. The Need for Genuineness
B. The Need for Effectiveness

Review
  I. A Disciple Does Not Fear the World (vv. 26-31)
 II. A Disciple Confesses Christ Before Others (vv. 32-33)

Lesson
III. A Disciple Puts Christ Before His Family (vv. 34-37)
    A. The Paradox of Christ's Coming (v. 34)
       1. Jesus did not bring peace
          a) Contrary to Jewish expectations
          b) Contrary to the disciples' expectations
       2. Jesus did bring division
          a) Old Testament teaching
          b) Rabbinic tradition
          c) New Testament reality
          d) Reformation history
    B. The Impact of Christ's Coming (vv. 35-37)
       1. Division between parent and child
       2. Division between man and family
       3. Division between husband and wife
IV. A Disciple Follows Christ Anywhere (vv. 38-39)
    A. The Call to the Cross (v. 38)
    B. The Call to a Choice (v. 39)
       1. A bad choice (v. 39*a*)
       2. A good choice (v. 39*b*)

V. A Disciple Brings Blessing to Others (vv. 40-42)
  A. Those Who Believe Receive the Gospel
  B. Those Who Believe Receive Rewards
    1. Because they receive God's people
    2. Because they help God's people

Conclusion

Introduction

President Theodore Roosevelt reportedly observed that never yet has a man led a life of ease whose name is worth remembering. He said, "I wish to preach, not the doctrine of ignoble ease, but the doctrine of the strenuous life" (Hamilton Club, Chicago, 10 Apr. 1899). The Lord does not call His disciples to a life of ease. The high calling of discipleship is perhaps most forcibly stated in Matthew 10:38-39, where Jesus says, "He that taketh not his cross and followeth after me, is not worthy of me. He that findeth his life shall lose it; and he that loseth his life for my sake shall find it." Jesus' instructions in Matthew 10:24-42 call for self-denial and self-sacrifice—a commitment to obey the divine will at any cost.

A. The Need for Genuineness

Many people claim to follow Jesus. But our Lord often spoke of the marks of a genuine disciple to expose those whose discipleship was only a facade. That distinction has often been overlooked in contemporary Christianity.

Speaking of Israel, the apostle Paul said, "They are not all Israel, who are of Israel" (Rom. 9:6). All who are outwardly God's covenant people are not so inwardly. Similarly, not all who are outwardly disciples of Jesus Christ are His disciples in their hearts. Matthew 10:24-42 gives us the marks of a genuine disciple.

B. The Need for Effectiveness

Matthew 10:24-42 also deals with the effectiveness of the disciple. Jesus was concerned not only with qualifications but also with how a real disciple affects his world and is af-

110

fected by it. Genuine disciples are to impact their surroundings.

Review

I. A DISCIPLE DOES NOT FEAR THE WORLD (vv. 26-31; pp. 84-94)

II. A DISCIPLE CONFESSES CHRIST BEFORE OTHERS (vv. 32-33; pp. 101-5)

Lesson

III. A DISCIPLE PUTS CHRIST BEFORE HIS FAMILY (vv. 34-37)

Jesus said that some who followed Him would be delivered up to councils, scourged in synagogues, and brought before governors and kings (Matt. 10:17-18). Those who were His true disciples would confess Him (Matt. 10:32), whereas those who were not would deny Him (Matt. 10:33). In Matthew 10:34-37 Jesus builds upon what He had already said to show that He would bring division.

A. The Paradox of Christ's Coming (v. 34)

"Think not that I am come to send peace on earth; I came not to send peace, but a sword."

1. Jesus did not bring peace

   a) Contrary to Jewish expectations

   At the time of Christ, the Jewish people expected that when the Messiah came He would bring peace. Isaiah said He would be the Prince of Peace (Isa. 9:6). Referring to the messianic kingdom, Psalm 72 says, "The mountains shall bring peace to the people" (v. 3). That psalm also says that in the Messiah's "days shall the righteous flourish, and abundance of peace

111

as long as the moon endureth" (v. 7). Isaiah 2:3-4 says, "Many people shall go and say, Come ye, and let us go up to the mountain of the Lord, to the house of the God of Jacob; and he will teach us of his ways, and we will walk in his paths; for out of Zion shall go forth the law, and the word of the Lord from Jerusalem. And he shall judge among the nations, and shall rebuke many peoples; and they shall beat their swords into plowshares, and their spears into pruning hooks; nation shall not lift up sword against nation, neither shall they learn war any more." Therefore Israel thought the Messiah was coming to bring peace.

b) Contrary to the disciples' expectations

Prior to Jesus' instruction in Matthew 10, His disciples had begun to experience the peace that comes from knowing Jesus. It is possible they expected that bliss to gain immediate acceptance throughout the world as they preached the gospel. Since the Messiah had come and He was the Prince of Peace, it would have been natural to assume that His kingdom rule was imminent.

2. Jesus did bring division

However, the immediate establishment of the messianic kingdom was not to be, and the Lord warned His disciples not to be under any illusions about His immediately inaugurating the kingdom of peace. Paradoxically, the Prince of Peace brought division and a sword. In the sovereignty of God it was necessary that the offer of peace with God result in division and strife.

a) Old Testament teaching

The Old Testament pictures the divisive nature of the Messiah's coming. Micah 7:6 says, "The son dishonoreth the father, the daughter riseth up against her mother, the daughter-in-law against her mother-in-law; a man's enemies are the men of his own house." That passage is almost directly quoted by our Lord in Matthew 10:35-36.

112

b) Rabbinic tradition

The divisiveness of the Messiah's coming was affirmed in rabbinic tradition. *Shabbath* 118*a* in the Talmud depicts the advent of the Messiah as being preceded by years of great distress. The rabbis were well aware of Micah 7:6.

c) New Testament reality

Jesus confirmed that His disciples could expect division—not peace. Rather than the incarnation of Christ bringing peace, the message the disciples proclaimed would split and fracture the world into segments and parties that would strive against one another. That is why we ought not to think that when we proclaim the gospel, everyone will line up to sign on the dotted line.

d) Reformation history

Martin Luther reportedly said that if our gospel were received in peace, it would not be the true gospel. He knew from experience how divisive the gospel can be. While he remained part of the Roman Catholic church he preached the truth, but it didn't bring peace. Rather it shattered the Roman Catholic church and gave birth to the Protestant Reformation.

The Paradox of the Prince of Peace

One would expect our Lord to bring peace. John the Baptist was the herald of Christ and announced the peace the Messiah would bring (Luke 1:76-79). The angels who proclaimed Christ's birth announced peace on earth (Luke 2:14). In John 14:27 Jesus says, "Peace I leave with you, my peace I give unto you." In John 16:33 He says, "These things I have spoken unto you, that in me ye might have peace. In the world ye shall have tribulation: but be of good cheer; I have overcome the world." In Romans Paul writes of the peace God has given us (Rom. 1:7; 5:1; 8:6; 14:17).

One who believes has peace in his heart, but in the world there is nothing but division. The Old Testament writers didn't understand the time span between Christ's first and second comings (1 Pet. 1:10-11). The first coming brought a sword, and the second coming will bring ultimate peace.

The gospel of peace is divisive. It is a refiner's fire, a separating of sheep and goats, and a winnowing of grain. If Christ had never come, the earth would have gone on in unity to hell, doomed for all eternity. The paradox of the Prince of peace is that when He came, war broke out.

B. The Impact of Christ's Coming (vv. 35-37)

"I am come to set a man at variance against his father, and the daughter against her mother, and the daughter-in-law against her mother-in-law. And a man's foes shall be they of his own household. He that loveth father or mother more than me, is not worthy of me; and he that loveth son or daughter more than me, is not worthy of me."

In Luke 12:49-53 Jesus says, "I am come to send fire on the earth; and what will I, if it be already kindled? . . . Suppose ye that I am come to give peace on earth? I tell you, Nay; but rather division; for from henceforth there shall be five in one house, divided; three against two, and two against three. The father shall be divided against the son, and the son against the father; the mother against the daughter, and the daughter against the mother; the mother-in-law against her daughter-in-law, and the daughter-in-law against her mother-in-law."

Perhaps the most devastating expression of the divisiveness Jesus can cause is seen in home relationships. Those are generally the most meaningful relationships in a person's life. But true disciples are committed to their Lord and are willing to exist, if necessary, in an environment of divisiveness in the place that ideally provides the greatest security and love.

The Greek word translated "at variance" is used only here in the New Testament. It refers to cutting something apart. Jesus said that the rending of relationships would extend from immediate family relationships to those by marriage.

1. Division between parent and child

   Such divisiveness is at odds with the natural love one feels as a parent or child. A strained relationship with a neighbor, boss, or friend is rarely as bad as strife with a family member.

2. Division between man and family

   Luke 9 records how a man pledged to follow Jesus but first desired to bid farewell to his family. Jesus said, "No man, having put his hand to the plough, and looking back, is fit for the kingdom of God" (v. 62). Jesus will not accept a disciple who is unwilling to break away from family ties for His sake.

3. Division between husband and wife

   Some wives will not come to Christ for fear of separation from their husbands, and some husbands reject Him because of their wives. Children often fail to come to Christ out of fear of their parents. Many people choose a comfortable family life in place of a living relationship with Christ.

   First Corinthians 7 deals with the reality of division in marriage when one partner comes to know Christ. The apostle Paul explained that a believing husband is to remain with his unbelieving wife if she desires to stay in the marriage and vice versa (vv. 12-13). In both situations the unbelieving partner is blessed: "The unbelieving husband is sanctified by the wife, and the unbelieving wife is sanctified by the husband" (v. 14). "But if the unbelieving depart, let him depart. A brother or a sister is not under bondage in such cases; but God hath called us to peace" (v. 15).

By becoming a Christian a person affirms his commitment to the lordship of Christ. That means a willingness to forsake all for Him. Raising your hand, signing a card, walking down an aisle, or saying, "I love Jesus" are one-time occurrences that in themselves do not demonstrate a life in union with Christ. Salvation is by faith in the finished work of Christ, but it does not occur without producing an unswerving commitment to obey Christ. It is a commitment so deep that a person will say no to the natural objects of their affection if loyalty to Christ so demands.

One Pilgrim's Family Predicament

Puritan John Bunyan knew what it meant to forsake his family for Christ. He was called by God to preach but was ordered by the government to stop preaching or be imprisoned. That meant he would be unable to support his family—they might lose their home and starve.

Nevertheless, he determined to obey God's call to preach and was imprisoned. He wrote in an appendix to his autobiography, *Grace Abounding to the Chief of Sinners*, "The parting with my Wife and poor Children hath often been to me in this place [of imprisonment], as the pulling the Flesh from my Bones; and that not only because I am somewhat too fond of these great Mercies, but also because I should have often brought to my mind the many hardships, miseries, and wants that my poor Family was like to meet with, should I be taken from them, especially my poor blind Child, who lay nearer my heart than all I had besides. O the thought of the hardship I thought my blind one might go under, would break up my heart to pieces. . . . But yet, recalling my self, thought I, I must venture you all with God, though it goeth to the quick to leave you; O I saw in this condition, I was a man who was pulling down his House upon the head of his Wife and Children; yet thought I, I must do it, I must do it" (cited by T. R. Glover, *Poets and Puritans* [London: Methuen & Co., 1915], p. 110).

As a result of Bunyan's predicament, God used him to bless millions of families. While in Bedford prison he wrote the Christian classic *The Pilgrim's Progress*.

Matthew 10:36 affirms that Christ came to bring a sword that would fall in the house. Verse 37 states plainly the high calling of discipleship and the choice that must be made. You can't be a disciple of Jesus Christ and participate in the salvation He offers if your family means more to you than He does.

IV. A DISCIPLE FOLLOWS CHRIST ANYWHERE (vv. 38-39)

A. The Call to the Cross (v. 38)

"He that taketh not his cross and followeth after me, is not worthy of me."

You may have heard devotionals about bearing or taking up your cross. You may have heard various definitions of what the cross might be—your spouse, teenager, in-laws, old Chevy, leaky roof, distasteful class at school, neighbor, boss, or any number of other things. But Jesus didn't mean any of that.

Also, He wasn't referring to His own crucifixion on Calvary. His disciples didn't yet understand that Jesus was going to be crucified (Matt. 16:21)—even after He told them He would be killed, they failed to accept that reality until it actually happened. So there was no mystical or devotional sense to what Jesus said.

When Jesus said to take up your cross, His disciples knew immediately what He was talking about. He was talking about dying. Those men, with the exception of Judas Iscariot, were from Galilee. When Jesus was about ten years old, Judas of Galilee and his followers revolted against the Romans and lost (Josephus, *Wars of the Jews* 2.8.1). To make an example that would not be forgotten, the Romans crucified more than two thousand Jews, placing crosses along the roads of Galilee. Everywhere people went they saw men dying on crosses along the roadside. And every Jew crucified carried the crossbeam for his own execution on his back as he marched to the cross. It was a lesson that could not be ignored.

Jesus impressed upon His hearers that those who follow Him must be willing to die a torturous death rather than deny Him. Crucifixion is the most excruciating death man has ever invented. Beyond the agony caused by nails driven through one's hands and feet, death itself comes by slow suffocation. The disciples understood that Jesus meant they were to be committed to the point of death. Jesus isn't the Savior of those who aren't committed to Him. The love of the Lord Jesus Christ must overrule the instinct for self-preservation.

B. The Call to a Choice (v. 39)

1. A bad choice (v. 39*a*)

"He that findeth his life shall lose it."

"Findeth his life" refers to securing one's physical safety by denying Christ under pressure. There are many kinds of pressure and many ways of denying Christ. But yielding to pressure and preserving one's life ultimately results in the loss of one's own soul.

2. A good choice (v. 39*b*)

"He that loseth his life for my sake shall find it."

Jesus didn't mean you get saved by being a martyr. Rather, if you are a genuine Christian you will be willing to die for Him. When given the choice between denying the Lord or denying yourself, you will deny yourself even to the point of death. He who confesses Christ and suffers death is far better off than the apostate who escapes death temporarily but receives eternal damnation.

When John Bunyan was brought before a judge and threatened with imprisonment for preaching without a license, he replied that obedience to Christ required that he do two things: actively obey Christ's commands to the utmost; and when threatened with punishment for such obedience, willingly suffer that punishment rather than refuse to obey Christ (cf. Glover, p. 110).

It is better to lose everything—your comfort, family, and life—and be hassled, intimidated, and badgered by the world than to forsake Jesus Christ. Not all of us will face that choice, but those who do will be proved true or false by whether they follow Jesus Christ or not, regardless of the cost.

V. A DISCIPLE BRINGS BLESSING TO OTHERS (vv. 40-42)

"He that receiveth you receiveth me, and he that receiveth me receiveth him that sent me. He that receiveth a prophet in the name of a prophet shall receive a prophet's reward; and he that receiveth a righteous man in the name of a righteous man shall receive a righteous man's reward. And whosoever shall give to drink unto one of these little ones a cup of cold water only in the name of a disciple, verily I say unto you, he shall in no way lose his reward."

A. Those Who Believe Receive the Gospel

Even though we often bring a sword that divides, we are also allowed to participate in the eternal salvation of God's people. When we preach the Word, live godly lives, and confess our Lord by our testimony, some will believe in Jesus Christ.

We have a limited ability to reward those who receive us and believe the gospel message. But the Lord has an unlimited ability and does that work for us. In verse 40, the Greek word translated "receive" refers to a full acceptance of the gospel message and the messenger who brought it. By receiving the message and the messenger, they are receiving the Lord Jesus Christ Himself.

In John 14:23 Jesus says, "If anyone loves me, he will obey my teaching. My Father will love him, and we will come to him and make our home with him" (NIV). When we preach the gospel, we participate in giving people the Trinity—the Father and the Son make their home in every believer by the indwelling Holy Spirit.

B. Those Who Believe Receive Rewards

1. Because they receive God's people

In Matthew 10:41 the term "prophet" refers to the task of those who proclaim the gospel. "Righteous man" refers to their character. Both terms refer to the same person. A true disciple declares God's truth and practices what he preaches.

When we represent God in word and deed and are received by those who adopt faith in Christ, they will receive the same reward we receive. Every disciple is promised not only future blessing but also acts as a means of blessing to those who receive their testimony.

Those who want to be a blessing in the world need to confess Christ before men. They need to be bold and not try to excuse their testimony or be ashamed of Christ. That kind of life becomes a source of reward for others.

2. Because they help God's people

When we think of prophets and righteous men, we generally picture high-class super-saints. But in Matthew 10:42 our Lord refers to His disciples as "little ones." Disciples are the Lord's "little ones"—not much in and of themselves. When they present the Lord Jesus and someone demonstrates his reception of the gospel by giving them a cup of cold water, the Lord will reward that helper. Those who receive the gospel are rewarded both when they believe the message and when they help the messenger in his work.

William Barclay recounts the story of a young man in a village who, "after a great struggle, reached the ministry. His helper in his days of study had been the village cobbler. The cobbler . . . was a man of wide reading and far thinking, and he had done much for the lad. In due time the lad was licensed to preach. And on that day the cobbler said to him, 'It was always my desire to be a minister of the gospel, but the circumstances of my life made it impossible. But you are achieving what was closed to me. And I want you to promise me one thing—I want you to let me make and cobble your shoes—for nothing—and I want you to wear them in the pulpit when you preach, and then I'll feel you are preaching the gospel I always wanted to preach standing in my shoes.' Beyond a doubt the cobbler was serving God as the preacher was, and his reward would one day be the same" (p. 399).

When a person receives a disciple who represents the Lord Jesus Christ, he receives the Lord Himself and will be rewarded, just as the disciple himself will be. By receiving the messenger of the gospel as well as the message itself, a person embraces the blessings and eternal gifts God gives to His own.

Conclusion

Disciples of Jesus Christ are involved in a fantastic enterprise. For many we are a source of conflict, for others a source of blessing. We must show all where they stand before God. That requires a commitment to follow Jesus Christ at any price.

In the depths of winter, Napoleon's army was retreating from its invasion of Russia. The army was pressed on all sides and had to cross the Berezina River to escape. The Russians had destroyed all the bridges, and Napoleon ordered that a bridge be built across the river. The men nearest the water were the first to attempt to carry out the almost impossible task. Several were carried away by the furious rapids. Others drowned due to the cold and their exhaustion, but more came and the work proceeded as quickly as possible. Finally, the builders completed the bridge and emerged half-dead from the icy water. As a result of that incredible effort, the French army marched across the Berezina River in safety (R. F. Delderfield, *The March of the Twenty-Six* [London: Hodder and Stoughton, 1962], p. 197).

That was an instance of heroic self-sacrifice. In a similar way, Christ calls His disciples to give their lives to build bridges for others to cross into the presence of God. If you're a true disciple, you will be willing to do just that.

Focusing on the Facts

1. What is perhaps the most forceful statement about the high calling of discipleship (see p. 110)?
2. Why did Jesus often speak of the marks of a genuine disciple (see p. 110)?

3. _____ disciples are to have an impact on their surroundings (see p. 111).
4. Why did the Jewish people at the time of Christ expect the Messiah to bring peace (see pp. 111-12)?
5. Paradoxically, it was the Prince of peace who brought _____ and a _____ (see p. 112).
6. What passage in the Old Testament pictures the divisive nature of the Messiah's coming (see p. 112)?
7. What lesson does the experience of Martin Luther demonstrate (see p. 113)?
8. What is the paradox of Jesus Christ, the Prince of peace (see pp. 113-14)?
9. What does the Greek word translated "at variance" in Matthew 10:35 mean (see p. 114)?
10. What passage in Scripture shows Jesus' attitude toward those unwilling to break away from family ties for His sake (see p. 115)?
11. Where did Paul write about the problem of Christians married to non-Christians? What were his instructions (see p. 115)?
12. Why aren't raising your hand, signing a card, walking down an aisle, or saying "I love Jesus" indications in and of themselves of a life in union with Christ (see pp. 115-16)?
13. What was Jesus referring to when He said that one must take up his cross and follow Him (see p. 117)?
14. Yielding to pressure and preserving one's life results in the loss of one's own _____ (see p. 118).
15. When Jesus said, "He that loseth his life for my sake shall find it" (Matt. 10:39), did He mean that only martyrs are saved? Explain (see p. 118).
16. According to John Bunyan, when a disciple is unable to actively obey Christ, what should he be willing to do (see p. 118)?
17. In verse 40, what does the Greek word translated "receive" refer to (see p. 119)?
18. In Matthew 10:41, to whom do the terms "prophet" and "righteous man" refer (see p. 119)?
19. For what two things are those who receive the gospel rewarded (see pp. 119-21)?

Pondering the Principles

1. Will the Lord receive as His own someone who once made a "decision" for Him but then lived a life that denied Him in word

and deed? In Matthew 10:32-33 our Lord says, "Whoever acknowledges me before men, I will also acknowledge him before my Father in heaven. But whoever disowns me before men, I will disown him before my Father in heaven" (NIV). Paul expresses the same thoughts in 2 Timothy 2:11-13. Puritan theologian John Owen wrote that Christ "cannot save unbelieving, impenitent sinners; for this cannot be done without denying Himself, acting contrary to His Word and destroying His own glory" (cited in *The Golden Treasury of Puritan Quotations*, edited by I. D. E. Thomas [Edinburgh: Banner of Truth Trust, 1977], p. 302). Do your words and deeds acknowledge Jesus Christ before men?

2. The author of Hebrews wrote that Christians are to "make every effort to live in peace with all men and to be holy; without holiness no one will see the Lord" (Heb. 12:14, NIV). In 1654 Thomas Brooks wrote, "Holiness is the very marrow and quintessence of [Christianity]. Holiness is God stamped and printed upon the soul; it is Christ formed in the heart; it is our light, our life, our beauty, our glory, our joy, our crown, our all. The holy soul is happy in life, and blessed in death, and shall be transcendently glorious in the morning of the resurrection, when Christ shall say, Lo, here am I, and my holy ones, who are my joy" (*Heaven on Earth: A Treatise on Christian Assurance* [Edinburgh: Banner of Truth, 1961 reprint], pp. 319-20). If you desire to follow Christ in accordance with Matthew 10:5-42, holiness of character in the power of the Holy Spirit will be the key to your success.

Scripture Index

126

127

Topical Index

call to, 11-14, 22
caution in, 62
charge of (*see* free charge of)
clarity in, 18-20
commission to (*see* call to)
contentment in, 32-33
credentials for, 25-31
dangers of, 39-68
effective, 7-38, 110-11
fee of (*see* free charge of)
free charge of, 29-31
frustration in, 18
message of the, 18-20
objective of, 14-18, 22
pastoral, 39-68
persecution in (*see* danger of)
provision of God in (*see* Provision of God)
receptivity and, 33-36, 38
training for, 10
traveling, 31-35, 65-66
See also Discipleship
Miracles, apostolic, 25-31
Missions. *See* Ministry

Napoleon, on the Berezina River, 121
Nightingale, Florence, on being thirty, 73

Offense, unnecessary, 61
Owen, John, on Christ's not saving the impenitent, 122-23

Peace, Jesus and, 111-16
Persecution
avoiding, 65-66
enduring, 64-65
family, 59-60, 67, 91, 111-16
government, 57-59, 67, 104
moving from (*see* avoiding)

provision of God (*see* Provision of God)
reality of, 45-60
religious, 55-57
responding to, 52, 60-68
See also Discipleship, of; Fear, of God *vs.* man
Perseverance of the saints, 64-65
Pliny the Younger, on genuine Christians, 104
Preaching. *See* Ministry
Prejudice. *See* Bigotry
Provision of God, 31-32, 37-38, 62-63, 93-96

Redaction criticism, error of, 72-73, 76
Rejection
open, 104
secret, 104-6, 122-23
Rewards, believers', 85-88, 119-21
Romans, the gospel according to, 48
Roosevelt, Theodore, on avoiding ease, 110
Ryle, J. C., on the cost of discipleship, 108

Salvation, confession and. *See* Confession, of Christ
Samaritans, ministry to, 15-16
Scourging, 55
Scripture, criticism of. *See* Redaction criticism
Second coming, turmoil preceding the, 111-16
Sempangi, F. Kefa, on Ugandan persecution, 58
Service, Christian. *See* Ministry